Woodpecker

Woodpecker

Gerard Gorman

REAKTION BOOKS

For Martin and Dominic

Published by
REAKTION BOOKS LTD
Unit 32, Waterside
44–48 Wharf Road
London N1 7UX, UK
www.reaktionbooks.co.uk

First published 2017
Copyright © Gerard Gorman 2017

Printed and bound in China by 1010 Printing International Ltd

A catalogue record for this book is available from the British Library

ISBN 978 1 78023 829 6

Contents

Introduction

Most people have probably never seen a real, live woodpecker of any kind and know very little about them. This is perhaps unsurprising as much of the life of the woodpecker goes on unseen, away from human eyes. Woodpeckers are enigmatic, often elusive, only briefly glimpsed before they shuffle out of sight behind a tree trunk or flee into the depths of a leafy woodland. If asked to describe or sketch a woodpecker, I would wager that most people – adults, small children, even birdwatchers and ornithologists who cannot draw – would come up with a bird with a fairly stocky body and a strong-looking pointed beak, clinging to the side of a tree trunk. It might also be shown making a hole. That would actually be a fairly accurate image of a typical woodpecker, as many do look and behave like that. There are, however, many that are not 'typical'. As we shall see, the global woodpecker family is very diverse.

For millennia the charismatic woodpecker has chipped away at and nestled into the human imagination. It has perhaps not been as common in legend and lore as some other birds, such as the owl and the eagle, but its unique behaviour and the distinctive ecological role that it fulfils have always attracted the attention of humankind. Indeed, the global reach of woodpecker symbolism is impressive. Since ancient times an extraordinary mythology has developed around the woodpecker, appearing as it does in

Northern flicker in Cuba in a classic, vertical, woodpecker pose.

7

the superstitions of the ancient Greeks and Romans, in the legends of indigenous Americans and Bornean tribes, and in old and new Europe. In most cultures the woodpecker was, and is, respected, often considered mysterious and sometimes even worshipped. Where it appears in mythology it is rarely a bit-part player and is, in fact, often a major protagonist. It has fulfilled a variety of roles, being symbolically associated with fertility, security, strength, prophecy, magic, medicine, rhythm, the weather, carpentry and as a guardian of trees and woodlands. It has been a war-totem, a fire-bringer, a weather-forecaster and a boat-builder. The woodpecker embellishes ancient artefacts and modern postage stamps. Yet its role is inconsistent. A perusal of attitudes and tales from around the world finds it portrayed as crafty and wise, but also naive or foolish; generous but sometimes miserly; spiritual yet earthly; loyal and devoted, but promiscuous; a hero and a villain; a healer and creator, but also a destroyer; both a good and a bad omen, and linked to life and to death. In particular, a sharp divide is apparent between Christian and animistic societies. All in all, the woodpecker is a paradox.

Since a famous cartoon woodpecker hammered his way into the popular media of the twentieth century, it has often been associated with eccentricity, although this bears no relationship to the behaviour of real woodpeckers. They are no crazier than any other bird and anyone who is familiar with them will know that they are often assertive and usually industrious – perhaps it is these characteristics that have endeared them to humankind. Woodpeckers are exceptional in the bird world in that they communicate with each other by mechanical means, drumming with their bills upon trees rather than singing. Although a few other birds excavate nest holes in trees, woodpeckers are the indisputable masters of this skill. A bird that can bore holes deep into timber, without sustaining injury, is surely a creature with super-strength. A bird that creates a safe and sheltered tree cavity in which to raise its family is one we should admire and learn from. A bird that has a strong pair bond, as most woodpeckers do, is to be respected.

Woodpeckers are certainly alluring but they have never been domesticated, unlike pigeons and fowl. Although many species are colourful they are unsuitable as cage birds and do not make good pets. Not only do they not sing like songbirds, they are difficult to house and, unlike parrots and corvids, they are almost impossible to tame. Their wild spirit means they are just a little too feisty to keep cooped up. Woodpeckers have attitude. They have seldom been specifically hunted for food (in the majority of cultures woodpeckers are not considered worth eating), although when woodpeckers appeared in front of hunters who were looking for other more traditional targets, they would probably have been shot. I have no personal experience of the latter, but by all accounts woodpeckers apparently do not taste that good.

I have been interested in wildlife, particularly birds, for as long as I can remember, but one April day some thirty years ago I had an encounter that focused my attention. I was walking through the woods above Budapest, just a few minutes from where I am sitting now as I write this. Suddenly, I heard a determined, solid knocking sound ahead of me. As I approached the source of the sound, a shower of sawdust wafted down onto the track before

Bennett's woodpecker, on a postage stamp from Zaire.

9

Black woodpecker: the biggest member of the family in Europe.

me, followed by a large woodchip. I looked up and there was a black woodpecker, whacking a hole in the grey trunk of a big beech tree. The bird was almost all black, except for a crimson crown – which indicated that he was a male – and a white eye which he briefly fixed upon me. He must have been nearly 50 cm (20 in.) long from the point of his ivory-coloured bill to the tip of his tail – by far Europe's biggest member of the woodpecker family. This magnificent bird, *Dryocopus martius*, paused, but then got back to work, too engrossed in his task to care about me. That is one of the appealing things about the woodpecker: once it gets going on a carpentry job, almost nothing stops it. In the weeks that followed I returned to that place many times. I observed the male being joined by the female, who participated in the excavation, and saw a pile of wood debris accumulate at the base of the tree. I watched the pair taking it in turns to disappear into their nest hole for hours on end as they incubated their eggs, then raised their brood, arriving with food and leaving with faecal sacs, and then watched the chicks poking their heads out of the hole, begging for more food. In late May the young birds fledged and headed off into the forest.

The woodpecker is integral to the natural heritage of our planet, but it is also part of our cultural heritage. In many cultures it was regarded as the spirit or god of the ancient forest, but today we threaten the woodpecker by destroying those same forests. Protecting the woodpecker and the places where it lives is critical not only for the diversity of the planet, but for our own intellectual, psychological and cultural needs.

1 The Woodpecker Family

In scientific terminology, woodpeckers are the Picidae, a family in the avian order Piciformes. According to DNA sequence analysis and morphological studies, woodpeckers are regarded as being most closely related to honeyguides (Indicatoridae), but also to barbets (Capitonidae, Megalaimidae, Lybiidae) and more distantly to jacamars (Galbulidae), puffbirds (Bucconidae) and toucans (Ramphastidae). It is thought that the order Piciformes began to evolve around sixty million years ago, in the Paleocene epoch, and that the family Picidae diverged from its relatives around fifty million years ago. Woodpeckers as we know them today are probably around five million years old and are usually grouped into three subfamilies: the wrynecks (Jynginae), the piculets (Picumninae) and the so-called true woodpeckers (Picinae). The true woodpeckers are in turn divided into five tribes.[1] In this book, I use the name 'woodpecker' to denote all members of the Picidae:

Family: Picidae (all woodpeckers)
Subfamilies: Jynginae (wrynecks), Picumninae (piculets), Picinae (true woodpeckers)
Tribes: Nesoctitini, Hemicircini, Campephilini, Picini, Melanerpini

Arizona woodpecker: a typical woodpecker, with a stocky body and stout bill.

The few known woodpecker fossils suggest that the Picidae originated in Eurasia, whence they dispersed to Africa, North America and finally to South America. The earliest fossil (the distal end of a tarsometatarsus) is thought to be more than 25 million years old, dating to the late Oligocene epoch; discovered in central France, it is named *Piculoides saulcetensis*.[2] The oldest New World fossil, from the late Oligocene or early Miocene of 20 to 25 million years ago, is a contour feather embedded in amber, found on Hispaniola. The oldest fossil from the African continent was discovered in South Africa and dates from the Pliocene, three to five million years ago. This was named *Australopicus nelson-mandelai* in honour of Nelson Mandela.[3] Most other woodpecker fossils are much more recent.

Despite several attempts to provide an authoritative classification of the woodpeckers, their taxonomy is still rather muddled, at times even contentious.[4] A thorough examination of the whole

William Hayes,
*Great Spotted
Woodpecker*,
c. 1780, etching.

family's evolutionary history is needed to fully understand the relationships among species.[5] Until recently, most taxonomic analysis was based on plumage features, on behaviour and ecology, or on morphology and anatomy. Today, most studies focus on DNA sequence analysis, the results of which suggest that similarities in the plumage and ecology of woodpeckers are due mostly to what is termed convergent evolution – the independent evolution of similar features in species of different lineages, or in lay terms, how different woodpecker species arrived at the same solutions to the ecological selection pressures they were faced with. There is not even agreement about how many woodpecker species there actually are.[6] Species limits (how species and sub-species are separated and categorized) are particularly unclear among the tiny piculets, but similar uncertainty persists in the case of some groups of larger and more familiar woodpeckers. The very existence of some species is doubtful. The total number of extant woodpecker species probably lies between 225 and 250. The most widespread woodpecker globally is *Dendrocopos major*, the great spotted woodpecker. First described by Linnaeus as *Picus major* in 1758, this species is a true woodpecker in every sense, and serves here to illustrate woodpecker scientific classification, as follows: class Aves; order Piciformes; family Picidae (woodpeckers); subfamily Picinae (true woodpeckers); tribe Melanerpini; genus *Dendrocopos*; species *Dendrocopos major*.

Woodpeckers are relatively widespread globally, being found on every continent except Antarctica and Australia-Oceania. They are also absent from the Arctic, Greenland, Madagascar and Hawaii, though some species, often endemic species, are found on continental islands. The greatest woodpecker diversity is found in South America, followed by Southeast Asia, with Africa comparatively underrepresented. The wrynecks have an Old World distribution and the piculets a pantropical distribution, occurring in Asia, Africa and, predominantly, South America. True woodpeckers are found across the family's entire worldwide range.

There is also great diversity in the environments used by various woodpeckers. Many are habitat specialists with very specific needs, but some are opportunistic generalists. As one would expect, most woodpeckers are arboreal, living in all kinds of woods and forests, from sea-level areas to those at high altitudes. They occur in hot and humid rainforests, cold taiga forests, plantations, orchards, urban parks, even in your own garden, and some have adapted to life in such sparsely wooded places as arid savannahs, upland grasslands and lowland deserts. Besides trees, some species also nest and feed in bamboo, cactus and even the ground.

Woodpeckers are generally stocky birds, with short legs, strong, stiff tails and robust, dagger-like bills. Although many woodpeckers do indeed fall into this category, readers with little

1

2

3

Delahaye, pinx! et lith.

A. Malherbe, direx!

DRYOPIC FAUVE, fig. 1, mâle, 2, femelle, 3, remige 4ͤ   DR. (Malh.) FULVUS. (Quoy et Gaim.)

previous knowledge of woodpeckers might be surprised at the family's rich diversity in appearance – and behaviour. Many species do not resemble the so-called true woodpeckers, the sub-family most people readily recognize as real woodpeckers, the birds that live life in the vertical, clinging to tree trunks. The Eurasian wryneck and the red-throated wryneck are the most atypical of all. They probably represent an old lineage of wood-peckers that branched off at an early stage from the one that eventually led to the true woodpeckers. With their thin bills, soft tails and slender bodies, they arguably look more like songbirds than woodpeckers. They also perch on branches rather than cling to trunks and do not excavate their own nest holes; indeed they

Banded woodpecker nesting in bamboo, Taman Negara, Malaysia.

Gila woodpecker nesting in cactus, Arizona.

Alfred Malherbe, 'Ashy Woodpeckers', from *Monographie des picidées* (1861).

Andean flicker,
Peru: a highly
terrestrial
woodpecker.

cannot, as they have not evolved the physical attributes to do so.
They do, however, have the characteristically long woodpecker
tongue. The piculets, which are most numerous in South America,
are the smallest woodpeckers, with many just 8–10 cm (3–4 in.)
long. Though they have many of the specializations that charac-
terize their larger cousins, such as long tongues, they have short
bills and soft tails. In Southeast Asia, the small, dumpy species in
the genera *Meiglyptes* and *Hemicircus* are often described as toy-
like. They appear big headed for their size and have short,
rounded tails. These species are sometimes regarded as inter-
mediates between the piculets and true woodpeckers. There are
also very large species – great slaty woodpeckers can reach more
than 50 cm (20 in.) in length.

There is diversity in colour, too, with some tropical woodpeckers, such as the yellow-fronted woodpecker in South
America and chequer-throated and crimson-winged woodpeckers in Southeast Asia, being almost gaudy. Others, however, such
as the smoky-brown woodpecker of Central and South America,
are rather plain. A few species are simply outlandish: the

Wryneck are atypical woodpeckers, often appearing songbird-like. This Eurasian wryneck was photographed in Croatia.

Lafresnaye's piculet, Peru. Piculets are the smallest woodpeckers.

blond-crested woodpecker of eastern South America sports a spiky crest and crown, and the female Magellanic woodpecker of Patagonia brandishes a curled, wispy crest of plumes. Most woodpeckers are sexually dimorphic (how males and females differ in plumage) in appearance, but the extent of the differences varies. An extreme case is the Williamson's sapsucker, the

male of which is strikingly marked black, white, yellow and red, while the very different female is mostly drab brown; the contrast is so great that early naturalists considered the two sexes different species. In a few species, for example middle spotted, red-headed and Guadeloupe woodpeckers, males and females are almost identical.[7]

Female Magellanic woodpecker in Chile showing its wispy crest.

Woodpecker behaviour is also diverse, and any attempt at generalization must be peppered with exceptions. Most species are monogamous, although somewhat antisocial outside the breeding season, but others are gregarious and live communally. The *Melanerpes* woodpeckers of the Americas include several highly social species, some with clan-based cooperative breeding systems that involve non-breeding helpers at the nest. The most studied of these is the acorn woodpecker, a species in which joint nesting by females sometimes occurs.[8] The red-cockaded woodpecker is another well-studied American species that raises its young cooperatively.[9]

Some of the family are not even called woodpeckers in English: there are sapsuckers, flickers, yellownapes and flamebacks. The four species of sapsucker all breed in North America. Though they do not actually suck tree sap, they do consume it, licking it up from purposely drilled holes called wells. Flickers are also New World woodpeckers. Three origins for their unusual English name have been suggested: the flickering of their bright wing

Hispaniolan woodpeckers, Dominican Republic: a highly social species.

colours when in flight,[10] the flicking in and out of their tongues when feeding, and an echoic one from their 'wicka' or 'wicker' contact call.[11] Many flickers forage on the ground for ants and termites, with the Andean flicker the most terrestrial of all, even excavating its nest hole in earth banks and occasionally adobe buildings. The greater yellownape and lesser yellownape in Southeast Asia are so called for the bright yellow on the back of their heads and necks. Also in Asia, the flamebacks (often called goldenbacks in India) are a group of true woodpeckers in the genera *Dinopium* and *Chrysocolaptes*. They acquired their colourful name due to the striking golden upperparts of most of the species (some are actually reddish or greenish above).

Despite this rich diversity, one thing that all woodpeckers have in common is that they are diurnal (active by day). Most woodpeckers are sedentary and live most of their lives in one place, although the young disperse before their first winter. Harsh weather and lack of food also sometimes prompt them to vacate an area and move further afield to survive. There are exceptions,

Black-rumped flameback, Chennai, India. Flamebacks are sometimes called 'goldenbacks'.

as ever, and a few species are decidedly migratory. Most of the European population of the Eurasian wryneck winters in Africa, and Asian populations in India. Rufous-bellied woodpeckers in northeast China and southeast Russia migrate to southern China for the winter, and yellow-bellied sapsuckers that nest in Canada and the northern USA fly as far as Central America and the Caribbean for the winter. Lewis's woodpecker, the northern flicker and red-breasted, red-naped and Williamson's sapsuckers also head south in autumn to the southern USA or Central America and return north in the spring.

In the folklore of Brittany in France, the woodpecker and the hoopoe (*Upupa epops*) are said to be close friends. A tale relates how these two birds once decided to fly across the sea in search of a new home, but the woodpecker tired and started to fall asleep. The hoopoe, however, kept his friend awake, not letting him drop into the waves below, by continually calling *oop-oop-oop, oop-oop-oop*. When the birds finally reached land, the woodpecker showed his gratitude by hacking out a hole in a tree for his friend to nest in. This is just a folk tale, but there is

Red-naped sapsucker at its sap wells, Oregon, USA.

ornithological accuracy here: hoopoes nest in tree holes, but are unable to excavate them themselves, and thus often use those created by woodpeckers. Although they did not use the term, the Bretons knew that the woodpecker was what modern ecologists call a 'keystone species'.

A keystone is a plant or animal that plays a major role in an ecosystem, helping to preserve its structure and affecting and even influencing many other organisms within it. Woodpeckers do this, albeit unintentionally, by providing tree cavities for other wildlife. They are 'primary cavity users'; that is, they make the holes they use for breeding. Those animals that use holes but

Seppo Leinonen, *Aspen and Inhabitants of Old Growth Forest*, 1996. This cartoon brilliantly illustrates the role woodpeckers play as keystone species.

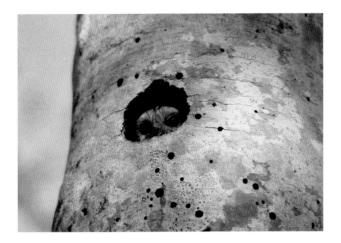

Bare-legged owl using an old woodpecker hole, Zapata Swamp, Cuba.

cannot make them are termed 'secondary cavity users'. Wood-peckers are ecosystem engineers, and the tree holes they create are in great demand. Some animals actually depend upon them; that is, without woodpeckers they would struggle to survive. Birds that nest in woodpecker holes include bluebirds, doves, ducks, flycatchers, honeyguides, owls, parrots, toucans, trogons, swal-lows, swifts, wrens and many more. Mammals such as bats, squirrels, dormice and martens all benefit from the work of wood-peckers, and even invertebrates such as wasps and bees move in when natural holes are lacking.

Because of the benefits they provide to other wildlife that share their habitats, and the fact that their requirements are similar to those of many other arboreal animals, woodpeckers can also be regarded as umbrella species. An umbrella species is one whose conservation can be expected to confer protection on many other co-occurring species.[12] Woodpeckers are also regarded as indica-tor species, which demonstrate the quality of an environment by their very presence.[13] They are excellent indicators of the health

of wooded habitats, and there is a clear correlation between their abundance and the richness of the forest and its other wildlife.[14] Diurnal and usually sedentary, woodpeckers can be considered as better indicator species than migratory birds, which are affected by conditions and circumstances elsewhere.

Though they serve as keystone, umbrella and indicator species, woodpeckers are only rarely the specific subjects of global conservation efforts. Instead, when habitat conservation is considered first, any benefit to the woodpeckers is secondary. But protecting woodpeckers protects many other wildlife species, and if woodpeckers disappear, many other species may well go with them.

Cuban green woodpecker, Zapata swamp, Cuba; some woodpeckers have adapted well to man-made urban habitats.

2 The Carpenter

In 1955 the BBC's *Look* series broadcast a short film entitled *Woodpecker* by the German wildlife film-maker Heinz Sielmann. The original title of this pioneering film was *Zimmerleute des Waldes*, literally 'Carpenters of the Forest'. For the first time, Sielmann took us into the nesting cavity of a pair of black woodpeckers deep inside a tree. With incredible ingenuity, he and his team engaged in a little carpentry themselves, cutting a section of trunk away and replacing it with a pane of glass through which the secrets of the entire breeding process could be captured on film. Great care was taken to habituate the birds and, after various trials and errors, film was obtained of the birds chipping at the chamber wall, incubating their eggs, feeding and brooding their chicks, removing droppings and, finally, the film-makers recorded the fledging of the young. Nearly four decades before the advent of modern digital photography, *Woodpecker* was a sensation, with a viewership rivalling that of the English FA Cup final. People who had never thought about woodpeckers of any kind, and journalists who usually focused on more trivial matters, swamped the BBC with requests for information.

The Spanish for woodpecker, *el pájaro carpintero* (the carpenter bird), perhaps sums it up. Barbets, relatives in the same Piciformes order as woodpeckers, also excavate holes in trees and some other birds will adapt existing cavities, but woodpeckers,

The impressive woodworking of a black woodpecker in search of carpenter ants in Estonia.

in any language, are the unrivalled master carpenters of the avian world. They exploit ecological arboreal niches that are beyond most other birds, indeed in the animal kingdom as a whole perhaps only beavers can rival their woodworking expertise. Around the globe, the woodpecker's remarkable ability to excavate nest holes in trees and hack into timber to find prey has fascinated humankind and led to their association with carpentry.

Aristotle describes, often remarkably, several distinct kinds of woodpecker and mentions the importance of the woodpecker's hard bill, its long tongue and even how some woodpeckers use 'anvils' to wedge and process nuts.[1] In his *Natural History*, Pliny the Elder observed that some woodpeckers could

climb straight up a tree, like a cat . . . cling to the tree upside down . . . and feel there is food under the bark by the sound it makes when they strike it. Woodpeckers are the only birds that raise their young in holes.[2]

Timber! Woodpeckers have been hard at work; Budapest, Hungary.

Foraging holes of the black woodpecker in Slovakia.

Given the era in which this was written, the knowledge that woodpeckers can 'feel' insect prey inside timber and tap trees to locate it is quite remarkable. Pliny was obviously a patient observer, one of the very first ornithologists, but the statement that they are the only birds to breed in cavities is not strictly true, as numerous other birds do so too.

Alexander Wilson, often said to be the father of American ornithology, learned at first hand about the phenomenal woodworking skills of the woodpecker. On a trip to collect an ivory-billed woodpecker specimen, he managed to wound a bird in the wing with his shot, and so took the poor creature back to his hotel in order to sketch it. Wilson left the woodpecker alone for a while in his room, but upon his return found that it had attempted to escape. Wilson was impressed and wanted the bird to survive, so he went to get food for it, this time tethering it by a leg to a table. Upon his return, he found that the spirited woodpecker had not given up on escape:

He had mounted along the side of the window, nearly as high as the ceiling, a little below which he had begun to break through. The bed was covered with large pieces of plaster; the lath was exposed for at least fifteen inches square, and a hole, large enough to admit the fist, opened to the weather-boards; so that in less than another hour he would certainly have succeeded in making his way through . . . As I reascended the stairs, I heard him again hard at work, and on entering had the mortification to perceive that he had almost entirely ruined the mahogany table to which he was fastened, and on which he had wreaked his whole vengeance.[3]

Warning! Woodpecker at work; Eifel National Park, Germany.

Clearly, woodpeckers are averse to being incarcerated, wasting no time in setting to work to hack their way to freedom. In his *Woodpeckers of Eastern North America*, Lawrence Kilham, who kept and successfully bred red-bellied woodpeckers in captivity, tells how he sought to resolve the problem of their inherent need to peck, chisel and excavate:

> Our aviary, on many mornings, sounded like a carpenter shop, as chips accumulated on the floor below . . . Keeping the woodpeckers supplied with hollow logs or bird houses for roosting at night was always a problem, for the woodpeckers often knocked them to pieces . . . All of these aviaries had to be lined with a tough plastic to protect the walls of the house. Woodpeckers love to dig into plaster, even on the ceilings.[4]

According to the creation myth of the Owambo people of Namibia, long ago people lived trapped inside a tree trunk, until a woodpecker answered their cries for help and used its bill to

Downy woodpecker throwing woodchips out as it works on its nest hole.

For the Ainu of Hokkaido and Sakhalin the woodpecker was the bird that made boats from logs.

open a hole through which they could emerge into the world.[5] The Bakiga and Banyankole people of Uganda leave us in no doubt at all about the importance of the woodpecker's bill: 'The woodpecker's bill is as strong as the spears of the Bachwezi and the day the bill dies marks the end of its life.' The Bachwezi were an ancient people said to have paranormal strength.[6]

The Bribri tribe of Costa Rica and Panama say that a man who excels at making canoes has been 'touched by the woodpecker'. The Ainu people of Hokkaido and the Russian island of Sakhalin called the woodpecker the boat-making bird. It was said to have been brought to earth by the god Aiona to teach people how to hollow out logs to make dugout canoes, but once the bird had taught them all he knew, the woodpecker was killed and eaten by Aiona in a ritual of respect. The Ainu kept woodpecker skins and heads as totems, used them in worship and believed that they brought wealth in addition to carpentry know-how. Unaware of the woodpecker's amazing anatomical adaptations, they called pains in the head 'woodpecker headaches', as they believed that the birds surely suffered from all their head-banging activity.[7]

In Greek mythology, Ascalaphus, the bird that sailed on the *Argo* with Jason, is usually considered to have been an owl; however, it has been suggested that it was actually a woodpecker with ship-building skills.[8] In Aristophanes' *The Birds*, the First Messenger declares to Pisthetaerus:

> Oh, there were bird carpenters too – the woodpeckers, naturally. Very skilful the way they split the timber for the gates with their beaks: and what a noise they made with their hacking and hewing – it sounded just like a shipyard![9]

Even today, joiners, cabinet makers and kitchen design companies readily incorporate the word 'woodpecker' into their names and business models, not only associating their products with quality woodwork but with 'natural' resources and the 'green' image that many consumers now demand and the woodpecker seemingly offers.

But how can a bird excavate timber? How can it repeatedly bang on and bore into trees without sustaining serious pain or injury?[10] The answers lie in the many remarkable physical adaptations woodpeckers possess. For all their attractions, woodpeckers are not generally regarded as graceful birds, but any absence of elegance is offset by their wonderfully functional physique; their anatomy has evolved to suit an arboreal life and, as we shall now see, some of those anatomical adaptations are extraordinary.

The axis of the bill is low on the woodpecker's thick skull, so the shock of striking hard surfaces when drumming or digging is transmitted to areas beneath the brain. A space between the skull and the brain filled with cerebrospinal fluid also reduces the potentially damaging force. Where the upper mandible meets the skull, a plate of spongy tissue functions as a shock absorber;

The Ainu of Hokkaido say a woodpecker first taught them how to carve canoes.

containing numerous tiny bony projections to help disseminate the force of impact, and when the birds are at work on hard surfaces the tissue curves inwards to reduce pressure on the brain.

Typical arboreal woodpeckers have straight, chisel-tipped bills made of hard but flexible bone – another impact-absorbing feature. Their bills are heavier than those of piculets and wrynecks, and more pointed than those of ground-feeding woodpeckers such as flickers, which have longer and more decurved bills. The importance of the bill is such that it grows quickly, appearing large and fully formed on nestlings even before their feathers emerge.

John J. Audubon,
'Ivory-billed
Woodpecker
Head Anatomy',
from *The Birds of
America* (1840).

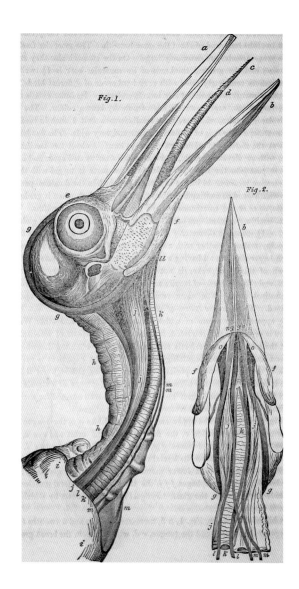

Green woodpecker
with its impressive
tongue extended.

Woodpecker tongues are astonishing, often three times the
length of the bill, and prehensile to a degree, useful for probing
holes and crevices for food. They are heavily barbed and sup-
ported by a long apparatus of bones, sinew and cartilage, called
the hyoid. Present in all birds, the hyoid is longer in woodpeckers
than most other birds, and the additional length means that the
tongue can be retracted and extended in and out of the bill. When
the tongue is retracted, the hyoid is wrapped around the skull and

Close-up of the barbed tongue of a black woodpecker.

fixed near the base of the upper mandible. This remarkable structure was commented upon by Aristotle and by Leonardo da Vinci, and has fascinated anatomists up to the present day.[11]

The woodpecker's skeleton is very robust, with muscles, ligaments and tendons, especially those attached to the ribs, thicker and stronger than in similar-sized birds. The second pair of ribs are particularly strong, as they support the scapulae, to which the neck muscles are attached. Interestingly, the neck muscles are more highly developed in the truly arboreal species than in those that tend to glean for food or forage on the ground. A large ploughshare-shaped bone, the pygostyle, at the end of the vertebral column provides attachment points for the shafts, or rachises, of the stiff central tail feathers. In true woodpeckers, which spend much of their time on tree trunks, those feathers act as props to keep their bodies off the trees' surfaces and to support the birds when they are stationary or shifting their feet. Piculets, which are gleaners, and wrynecks, which are mainly terrestrial foragers, do not have such strong tail feathers.

Woodpeckers' feet and toes are sturdy and scaly, with strong claws that function like crampons and are ideal for clinging to and climbing up trees. Most perching birds have anisodactyl feet, an arrangement in which three toes point forwards and one toe, the hallux, points backwards. In most woodpeckers, the foot is zygodactyl, with a so-called yoked arrangement in which the

Grey-headed woodpecker extending its long tongue.

Woodpecker skeleton model by Martin Vitek, 2012, on display in hall 32 at the Natural History Museum, Vienna.

West Indian woodpecker clinging to a vertical wall with its feet and using its tail as support, Cuba.

Pale-billed woodpecker using its claws like crampons, Costa Rica.

fourth toe, the hallux, is rotated outwards; in large woodpeckers, however, the hallux may move in a lateral direction. Inevitably, there are exceptions, and some woodpeckers, such as the appropriately named Eurasian and American three-toed woodpeckers, and bamboo and pale-headed woodpeckers in Asia, are tridactyl, with just three toes on each foot.

Besides these major adaptations, woodpeckers have also evolved many subtle, less obvious bodily modifications, such as a gland at the base of the skull that secretes fluid believed to trap the wood dust produced when excavating trees; narrow nostril slits covered by bristles that also prevent dust from entering the

Banded woodpecker excavating a nest hole in an old bamboo, Taman Negara, Malaysia.

head; and a nictitating membrane that closes over the eye to protect it just before the impact of any debris, although the last is not unique to woodpeckers. The inner ear has a thick membrane to resist damage, while a tough skin is a defence against wood splinters and the chemical sprays and bites of ants.[12]

Although their anatomical attributes have become better understood, the question is still asked: 'Why don't woodpeckers get headaches?' In recent years, this question has been repeatedly hammered out in popular culture and social media, and even on some semi-scientific forums, as the shock-absorbing anatomy of woodpeckers has received increasing attention and become a growing subject of study, particularly in the field of biomimicry. Scientists and designers are increasingly interested in determining how the wonders of woodpecker anatomy can be incorporated into the likes of crash-test dummies, protective helmets and collars for athletes, and aircraft black box designs (a black box built after studying woodpecker anatomy was apparently sixty times more protective than existing models).[13] It has been calculated that when excavating a hole, a woodpecker can tolerate impacts around sixteen times greater than humans without suffering injury.[14] The skull of a drumming woodpecker can experience shocks in excess of 1,200 g (force); to put this into perspective, humans suffer concussions at deceleration rates of less than 100 g. Hence some neurosurgeons researching brain injuries sustained by American football players are also looking at the woodpecker's physique. There is something, though, that is usually overlooked in popular accounts: woodpeckers are not indestructible. They can bang on trees all day long, and are able to tolerate much greater g-forces than humans, but they cannot sustain all impacts and often die when they fly into glass doors and windows. They rarely recover and fly away because their anti-concussion features, such as the fortified skull, have evolved to withstand the specific impacts sustained when *they* drum and peck on and hack into wood, and to protect *their* bodies, bones and brains when doing so.

Although woodpeckers have undeniable physical advantages, it would be a mistake to think that those attributes have evolved and exist at the expense of intelligence. In fact, woodpeckers are far from bird-brained. For example, the great spotted woodpecker

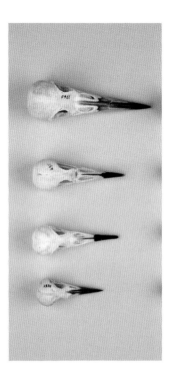

Woodpecker skulls and beaks. From top to bottom: black, green, northern flicker and great spotted.

has around 1.6 times more brain volume than the similarly sized Eurasian blackbird (*Turdus merula*).[15] The brains of true woodpeckers are well developed, ranking among the biggest in the avian world, right up there with crows, owls and parrots; indeed, woodpeckers have outperformed parrots in some experiments on intelligence. We know of the 'wise owl', but we never hear of the 'wise woodpecker', although there was a nod in the direction of the sagacious woodpecker in the 1970s, in the British children's television series *Bagpuss*, which featured a character called Professor Yaffle, a spectacled wooden woodpecker bookend allegedly based upon the philosopher Bertrand Russell.

Woodpeckers spend most of their day foraging, and it is here that their intelligence and spatial memory are best revealed. The act of extracting concealed food is considered to require more intelligence than simply collecting readily available food from a surface, and woodpeckers show acumen and innovation when searching for and extracting prey from inside wood. They do not simply hack into the wood in a crude manner to see what is inside; rather, they are discerning and particular about where they forage. In experiments where food items are visible but concealed behind glass, woodpeckers have been observed to quickly solve the problem of accessing the reward without simply trying to break the glass.[16] Abundant food resources, such as ant and termite colonies, forests invaded by beetles and trees that are fruiting or where the sap is rising, are memorized and visited repeatedly. Yet these abundant food resources are not always depleted. In South Africa the terrestrial ground woodpecker

Professor Yaffle from the British TV series *Bagpuss*.

forages in social groups that systematically harvest anthills, not entirely exhausting the food source but rather allowing the ants to recover from the raids in an apparent example of sustainable use.[17] Woodpeckers are essentially insectivores, although some are fairly frugivorous, but most are also opportunistic, quickly adapting to local abundances in food and taking advantage of unanticipated nutrition resources. The likes of carrion, live reptiles, small mammals and even the chicks and eggs of other birds are eaten. Sapsuckers have been observed deliberately dipping insects into the sap oozing from their sap wells before feeding them to their chicks. Such resourcefulness (we might call it craftiness) certainly suggests intelligence. The New World genus *Melanerpes* includes several species that cache food. A spectacular example of such hoarding is exhibited by acorn woodpeckers, which create large stores of acorns and other nuts in trees and even wooden buildings. These diligent woodpeckers usually drill a specific hole for each differently sized item, inserting and wedging it so neatly and tightly that it is often hard for a human to

The Jamaican woodpecker is one of the many woodpeckers that readily eat fruit.

Acorn woodpecker granary, Arizona.

remove. Furthermore, as each acorn dries and shrinks, the birds will return to modify the fit of each hole to maintain the integrity of their store. Acorn woodpeckers are gregarious birds, and these stores, called granaries, are often the work of several individuals in a clan, and can contain thousands of items.

Several species of woodpecker create and maintain anvils, also known as smithies or workshops. These are cracks or crevices in trees, stumps, fence-posts or walls, where large or hard objects, such as conifer cones, nuts and hard-bodied insects, are brought and wedged in before being hacked open.[18] Some anvils are regularly used and piles of discarded debris, such as opened cones or cracked nutshells, accumulate on the ground below after having been deliberately removed. Other anvils are used just once, with a bird wedging and processing an item at an available site and then leaving the remains in place. Rather than simply forcing an item into an anvil, woodpeckers carefully examine the size and

Woodpecker anvil with discarded conifer cones in Finland.

Woodpeckers use anvils to work on conifer cones and other food items.

48

Woodpecker anvil
with a wedged nut.

shape of the object brought before considering the best way to
fit it into the anvil. Sometimes anvils are customized, enlarged
or shaped in order to fit the dimensions of the food item. All in
all, woodpeckers do not try to fit round pegs into square holes.
When working on an anvil, the bill functions as a multi-purpose
tool, at any one time a chisel, hammer, hatchet or crowbar.
Indeed, anvil use and anvil modification are a form of tool use, a
behaviour often thought of as an indication of intelligence in

animals. In Europe, great spotted and Syrian woodpeckers are the most regular users of anvils, and in North America, the red-headed woodpecker routinely wedges food items. Woodpeckers do not, however, limit their brain power to matters of nutrition. As we shall soon see, some also show intelligence in the realm of communication.

3 The Drummer

Hearing a chorus of songbirds is glorious, and much celebrated, but the resonating rhythm of the woodpecker's drum touches upon something deeper – anyone who has walked in a woodland on a spring morning and heard the volleyed tattoo of a woodpecker drumming on timber will understand. There is something inherently primal about it. Drums are the primordial musical instrument and drumming the spiritual essence of communication and music. For many people drumming embraces deep symbolic meanings, inspiring passion, fear and courage, and hence in many ancient (and some modern) cultures it is, often together with dance, intrinsic to rituals and ceremonies that focus on birth, death, marriage, healing, rites of passage and war preparations. Drumming was one of the very first long-distance modes of communication that ancient peoples used to herald events, send out invitations, warn of danger and issue threats. Woodpeckers drum for the very same reasons. Drumming is just one of the many ways in which people related to, and connected with, woodpeckers.

But what is woodpecker drumming? Perhaps we should start by explaining what it is not. Drumming has nothing to do with the hacking, pecking, chiselling and tapping sounds that woodpeckers make when foraging or excavating cavities in trees; although they might suggest drumming, such sounds are random

*Blue Tunes –
Animals Play Jazz
in Lapland*, by
cartoonist and
environmentalist
Seppo Leinonen.
Of course, the
woodpecker is on
the drums!

and much slower. Unlike foraging and excavating, drumming does
not result in any significant visible marks on the surface drummed
upon. It is a mechanical, instrumental, non-vocal method of communication which in the avian world is perhaps unique to
woodpeckers. Some barbets, which are relatives of woodpeckers,
might also drum or at least make tapping sounds for the same
purpose. It is the sound produced by a series of very rapid,
repeated strikes with the bill on hard surfaces. Woodpeckers do
not sing in the sense that songbirds do, but they do call and drum
in a rhythmic manner to communicate. Drumming therefore
might be regarded as serving the same purpose as song, but it
is relatively simple and less complex than most birdsong.[1] At

the end of the nineteenth century the American naturalist Fannie Hardy Eckstorm poetically explained it like this:

> Other birds woo their mates with songs, but the woodpecker has no voice for singing. He cannot pour out his soul in melody and tell his love his devotion in music … He is the only instrumental performer among the birds; for the ruffed grouse, though he drums, has no drum.[2]

When explaining what drumming is to children (and occasionally even to adult birdwatchers) I like to use the following analogy. When a woodcutter chops wood with an axe, he is not making music, he is working. His actions produce sounds, but they are haphazard, they are not rhythmic; the woodcutter's intention is only to cut timber. On the other hand, when a drummer hits his drum-kit with his drumsticks, the sounds he makes are rhythmic, he is making music, deliberately making sounds. When a woodpecker makes a nest hole or opens up timber to get at prey, it is as a woodcutter; when drumming, it is as a musician.

Each species has a diagnostic way of drumming and it seems that woodpeckers recognize the drumming of their own kind. Fascinatingly, different woodpecker species sharing the same environment are able to recognize their own species' drum roll based on the cadence (rise and fall) of the drumming. Experiments using recordings of the drumming of northern flickers played back to Nuttall's woodpeckers in the u.s. demonstrated that it was possible to illicit a response in the Nuttall's, because the cadence of the drumming from the flicker was similar. The explanation provided by the researchers involved was that of 'temporal separation' across the breeding season.[3] This is likely to be an evolutionary adaptation for different woodpecker species to enable them to share a similar woodland habitat by shifting the period when they drum. It allows them to co-evolve similar acoustical patterns, and for the most part the separation of the drumming period avoids confusion, but perhaps not for birders trying to identify the birds by sound. It may also be the case that individual woodpeckers are able to recognize the drumming of other individuals of their species, although this has not been proved.

Not all species drum to the same degree: some are avid percussionists, some seldom drum, others only weakly, and some, such as the wrynecks and the Antillean piculet, never drum. Size does not matter. The great slaty woodpecker of Asia is, presuming the ivory-billed and imperial woodpeckers are extinct, the largest woodpecker on the planet, at around half a metre (2 ft) long from the tip of its long bill to the end of its tail, but it does not drum. At the other extreme, many of the miniscule piculets of South America produce surprisingly loud, rapid, rattling rolls on bamboo. The drumming of some species starts slowly before speeding up, in others it is the opposite. Some produce smooth rolls of even tempo while the drumming of others is disjointed or, to continue the music theme, staccato. Typical drum volleys of the black woodpecker, for example, are comprised of powerful two to three second bursts of drumming each comprising fifteen to twenty strikes per second. The tempo of such long and loud drum rolls often suggests a machine-gun salvo. The rufous woodpecker of Southeast Asia makes very distinctive knocking rolls of up to five seconds each, which decelerate before grinding to a halt like a misfiring motorbike or stalling engine. Also found in Southeast Asia, pale-headed and bamboo woodpeckers produce loud, far-carrying rolls when they drum on the hard, hollow stems of old bamboo, which seem to rattle and then creak as the drumming slows down. The drum of the bearded woodpecker of sub-Saharan Africa is a measured, almost automated roll of around twelve hits

Africa's bearded woodpecker produces a slow, almost mechanical drum roll.

per second which stutters and falters towards the end before concluding with several solid, clear knocks. Most of the big *Campephilus* species in the Americas produce rather simple, but loud and solid, far-carrying, double (sometimes triple) knocks or raps on trees or logs rather than drum rolls proper – the first strike is so rapidly followed by the second that it often sounds like it has been hit with an echo.[4] In parts of Latin America, such as Costa Rica and Venezuela, the tiny piculets are called *telegrafistas* because the sound of their rapid, tinny drumming, and the sounds they make when foraging on vines, brings to mind the tapping that telegraphers made when sending messages.

Drumming is an important way of communicating with rivals and potential mates. It is both competitive and communicative, being at various times a deterrent and an attraction, a warning to others and an invitation. In some species pairs and rivals will indulge in long-distance communication; in others, such as the red-cockaded woodpecker in the southeastern u.s., it seems only to serve as a short-distance courtship gesture between males and females. This may be due to the fact that this species lives mainly on living pines, which when drummed upon do not resonate well and the resultant dull drum rolls do not carry far.[5] Woodpeckers sometimes start to drum when they are alarmed, and when the time comes for young woodpeckers to leave their nests, parents will encourage their offspring to leave their sanctuaries by drumming nearby. However, drumming is mostly associated with territorial behaviour in spring and, as a general rule, males tend to drum much more than females. In spring some males will drum several hundreds of times per day to impress females and to declare to other males that a territory is claimed. As Heinz Sielmann wrote in his book *My Year with the Woodpeckers* (1959):

> This drumming is the most significant of the woodpecker's activities, for it is an invitation to a female of the species to join him in boring a nesting hole, and a declaration to rival males that he owns the territory around it.[6]

In certain circumstances woodpeckers will drum almost anywhere, but most have favourite places where they drum, called drumming posts. These are often tree snags or dry branches that have good acoustic properties and which resonate well, amplifying the sound of the drum when struck. There are usually several of these posts within a woodpecker's homerange. As already mentioned, woodpeckers are intelligent, adaptable birds, and some urban-dwellers quickly worked out that satellite dishes, tv antennas, metal signs, utility poles, drainage pipes, gutters and other man-made structures are even better than wood for transmitting their drumming. Experience had shown them that their drumming would be louder and carry further from these metallic surfaces than from tree snags. Clearly, when the aim of your drumming is to declare your presence to rivals and potential mates, the bigger the noise you make, the better. This behaviour is a habit acquired in relatively recent times, as such structures obviously did not exist when woodpeckers first evolved. It is not, however, something they learned very recently, in the modern era, as woodpeckers were observed drumming on some artificial structures almost as soon as they were erected in nineteenth-century America. As Eckstorm put it,

> The woodpeckers very quickly discover the superior conductivity of metals. In parts of the country where woodpeckers are more abundant than good drumming trees, a tin roof proves an almost irresistible attraction. A lightning-rod will sometimes draw them farther than it would an electric bolt; and a telegraph pole, with its tinkling glass and ringing wires, gives them great satisfaction.[7]

Lafresnaye's piculet: a *telegrafista*.

Black woodpecker on its drumming post, a dry snag, in Hungary.

Referring in particular to the red-headed woodpecker, the same author wrote: 'He is the one that raps so merrily on your tin roofs when he feels musical.'[8] Anyone who has been roused at dawn by the loud rattling of a woodpecker drumming outside their bedroom window might not agree with Eckstorm's use of the word 'musical'. Fortunately, most woodpeckers only drum for a short period in the spring, ceasing when their territory is established, rivals have been seen off and a mate has been found. They seem to know, too, that the sound they make carries further from lofty locations as they usually choose spots high up on tall trees. Black woodpecker drumming, for example, can travel up to 3 km (2 mi.) through the forest when performed on high, exposed posts.[9] Calls do not travel as far. These canny birds have also realized that no matter how high up they are, or how good a drumming post resonates, drumming on windy days is largely a waste of time, so woodpeckers seldom do.

People, ancient and modern, have been fascinated by the drumming of woodpeckers. It has often been used as a symbol and looked upon as mysterious, as involving great power, sometimes supernatural strength, and associated with spirits and a call to arms. In some cultures, drumming woodpeckers heralded the onset of the rainy season or warned of approaching storms. Mighty thunder gods and thunder birds, which embodied the power of the heavens, existed in various forms in ancient cultures on every continent, but truth be told, few seem to have been based on the woodpecker. An exception was Zeus in Greek mythology, and in Norse legends the drumming of the woodpecker was associated with thunder and hence with the god Thor, son of Odin. The mythical thunderbirds that feature in many North American native tribal cultures were said to produce thunderclaps when they beat their huge wings. Unlike those in European legends, these imposing creatures were not based on woodpeckers, although it might be tempting to say so. The thunderbirds depicted on totem poles in the Pacific Northwest, for example, typically resembled eagles or ravens. This is perhaps surprising as in most global cultures where woodpeckers feature, their drumming was invariably linked to thunder and sometimes lightning, and they were significant birds in the mythologies of the Northwest tribes.

Many tribes knew that woodpeckers drummed on trees with their bills to speak with others of their kind, and the tribes associated this with how they themselves communicated to others by using their ceremonial wooden drums. In animistic cultures the drumming of woodpeckers has been considered nature's pulse, the primordial heartbeat of the earth. The rhythm hammered out

by the woodpecker on a tree was mimicked by the shaman on his
drum and led him through his ceremonial journeying. For some
American tribes the woodpecker is the totem of drummers and
all those who work with rhythm. The Taíno, who inhabited Caribbean islands such as Cuba, Hispaniola and Puerto Rico when
Columbus arrived in the New World, revered a woodpecker called

Inriri Cahubabayael.[10] This sacred woodpecker was believed by some to have shown people how to tap and beat out rhythms on the very first primitive *mayohuacán* drums, which they had made from hollow sections of logs and which resembled the cavities woodpeckers excavated in trees. The Bribri people of Costa Rica also say that the spirit of the woodpecker was the original drum-maker. The Tacana still live in Bolivia's Andean rainforests, where, before Europeans arrived, they were hunter-gatherers. In one of their myths a woodpecker (no particular species is mentioned) drums on a clay pot that belongs to a woman whose husband is lost deep in the jungle – the bird communicates with the man by drumming and guides him safely home. On the other side of the world, however, in the very heart of Europe, the opposite to this notion of the woodpecker as a guide was believed. Bohemia has been home to Germanic and Slavic peoples for centuries and wood-peckers feature widely in the folklore of the region: Grimm wrote that both Germans and Slavs traditionally regarded the wood-pecker as sacred.[11] Despite this, some Bohemians alleged that the black woodpecker drummed to deliberately mislead people into

Wall plaque of endemic Puerto Rican birds, with the Taíno people's sacred woodpecker at the centre.

Replica of a Taíno *mayohuacán* drum, made by Hailie Rivera, Puerto Rico.

thinking that woodcutters were at work and anyone who followed the sounds would lose their way deep in the forest. Quite why the woodpecker would do that is unclear, since in most myths and tales from the very same region the woodpecker is portrayed as a benevolent bird.

4 The Mythical Woodpecker

Wherever they occur, woodpeckers have been admired, respected and sometimes even worshipped. They have often been used symbolically, associated with such primal concerns as light, fire, water, divination, power and sex. As woodpeckers are arguably rather familiar birds, some of the extraordinary symbolism and myth that has been attached to them may come as a surprise.

Even those, like me, who have only a rudimentary knowledge of Roman mythology have heard the story of the abandoned infants Romulus and Remus, the founders of Rome, who were discovered and suckled by a she-wolf. What is not as widely known, however, is that a woodpecker joined the wolf in feeding the twins, opening the mouths of the boys and dropping in morsels of food as if they were chicks. Plutarch wrote: 'While the infants lay there, history tells us, a she-wolf nursed them, and a woodpecker constantly fed and watched them.'[1] Ironically, Ovid was not to know that the bird would be omitted from many subsequent accounts when he wrote 'Who doesn't know that the foundlings grew on wolf's milk and a woodpecker often brought them food?'[2]

Exactly when the role played by the compassionate woodpecker in the legend, and hence in the founding of the great city, was eclipsed by that of the wolf is unclear. Perhaps it is the absence of a woodpecker in the evocative bronze sculpture – in the Musei

Peter Paul Rubens, *Romulus and Remus*, 1615–16, oil on canvas. Note the three great spotted woodpeckers.

Capitolini in Rome – of the twins suckling from the she-wolf which is responsible for its exclusion. Certainly, that artwork is the one that most people seem to associate with the story. Three great spotted woodpeckers do feature in Rubens's painting of the same scene in the Musei Capitolini, and a bird (actually more like a magpie than a woodpecker) is present in Carracci's sixteenth-century painting of the scene in the Palazzo Magnani in Bologna. Nevertheless, it is the she-wolf rather than the woodpecker that has prevailed. As we shall see, although its role in the Romulus and Remus legend has been overlooked in most modern accounts, the Roman woodpecker was not the first of its kind to feature in the ancient mythologies of the Mediterranean. It was a significant

64

symbol in the Graeco-Latin region well before Rome was officially founded in 753 BC.

In ancient Persia and Babylon, the wryneck was considered to be closely associated with the godhead. Images of four golden wrynecks in the Babylonian court were apparently there to occasionally remind the king to be humble.[3] A green-coloured woodpecker appears in Mesopotamian mythology as the axe of Ishtar, and as worship of this multifarious goddess of war, desire, fertility and rebirth spread, including to Greece, so did the associations of the bird with these pagan themes. Greek mythology is riddled with woodpeckers. Early Minoans on Crete associated the bird with Zeus, the father of the Gods, and in Aristophanes' comedy *The Birds* a woodpecker reigned over the earth until Zeus deposed him. As Euelpides says to Pisthetaerus: 'You'd better keep your beaks well sharpened: I can't see Zeus handing over his sceptre to a woodpecker – especially if it's been making holes in his sacred oaks.'[4]

In his *Metamorphoses* (dated to sometime between AD 100 and AD 300 and not to be confused with Ovid's work of the same name) Antoninus Liberalis relates how King Celeus of Eleusis tried to steal honey intended for the infant Zeus from bees in a cave on Mount Ida. Rather than simply slaying Celeus and his cohorts in the sacred place of his birth, Zeus transformed them into birds – Celeus became a green woodpecker. Today *Celeus* is the name of a genus of striking Neotropical woodpeckers, although none are green. In another, typically rather complicated story involving abduction, rape, murder and cannibalism, Zeus punished several characters by changing them into birds. In this instance, the carpenter Polytechnos became a green woodpecker.[5] Given his trade, it is hard to think of a more appropriate bird for the ill-fated character.

Woodpeckers were also sacred to several other deities, such as Ares, the god of war. The parenthood of the nature deity Pan is disputed, but some sources mention that he actually hatched from a woodpecker's egg.[6] Others say that he was the product of a union between Hermes and Dryope, the daughter of King Dryops. The Greek *dryops* is interpreted as 'oak-face' or sometimes just as 'woodpecker', and today a genus of large woodpeckers is named *Dryocopus*, literally 'oak-cutters'.

With so many divine woodpeckers in ancient Greece it is not surprising that superstitions developed around them. One involved the unfortunate wryneck, which was believed to lure its main prey, terrestrial ants, into its bill by lying down on the ground and playing dead (in reality it licks up ants with its long tongue while very much alive). It was also believed that this ability could be harnessed by spurned lovers to lure back and charm wayward partners by means of a gruesome ritual. Wrynecks were caught and impaled upon small wheels which were spun around and made a humming sound. Such enchanted wryneck wheels were often ornate, with one supposedly created by the goddess of love, Aphrodite, that was said to have been finely gilded. Legend has it that Aphrodite used such a wheel to force Medea,

Chestnut-coloured woodpecker, a member of the *Celeus* genus.

a sorceress herself, to fall in love with Jason (of Argonaut fame). In yet another legend the nymph Iynx had her voice taken away by Hera, queen of the gods, who gave it to another nymph, Echo. Iynx sought revenge by casting a spell to make Hera's husband Zeus fall in love with the priestess Io (another mythical character to whom woodpeckers were sacred). When Hera learned of what Iynx had done, she cursed her and turned her into a wryneck; this legend resulted in some Greeks associating this woodpecker with sensuality and eroticism. The modern scientific name of the wryneck genus *Jynx* would later be derived from the ill-fated Iynx's name. Philyra, a shape-shifting goddess associated with healing, divination, beauty and perfume, is also traditionally allied to the wryneck, and the bird was an icon for a college of priestesses who served Thetis, yet another deity with powers of transfiguration who is usually associated with the sea or water in general. There are several versions of these legends, as well as descriptions of the protagonists, and things can become a bit convoluted, but one thing is fairly consistent – it was usually no fun being a wryneck in classical Greece.

The Picenes (also known as the Piceni) lived in Picenum (today's Marche and Abruzzi regions of central Italy) between the ninth and third centuries BC. They are one of the least-known pre-Roman tribes of the Italian peninsula, but a legend relates how their ancestors arrived from the east across the Adriatic in search of new lands. Almost as soon as they had disembarked, a green woodpecker perched on one of their banners – an act they took to be a good omen. They then followed the bird to the banks of the River Tronto, where it stopped and began to excavate a nest hole. This was interpreted as a sign to settle at that very spot, which they did, adopting the woodpecker as their sacred symbol and tribal totem. In some versions of this myth it was the woodpecker Picus that actually led the Picenes and from whom they

Woodpecker emblem of the Marche region in Italy.

Ascoli Picchio FC badge.

Woodpecker plaque on a wall in Pescasseroli, Abruzzi, Italy.

took their name.[7] Today's town of Ascoli Piceno is thought to have risen at the site where the Picenes settled, and a green woodpecker adorns the coat of arms of the Marche region. Even the local football club is called Ascoli Picchio FC (Ascoli Woodpeckers FC). The pagan woodpecker past of this part of Italy is also evoked in a colourful festival, the Sciò la Pica (the woodpecker chase), in the quaint hill town of Monterubbiano each Whitsun (Pentecost), where a woodpecker (though these days another bird is used to represent a woodpecker) is carried through the streets in a cage tied to a cherry tree branch.

Roman culture was, of course, influenced by the various peoples who already lived on the Italian peninsula. The subsequent cult of Picus may well have derived from the Picenes, but the greatest overall influence on Rome came from the Greeks, and the Roman counterparts of the Greek gods usually inherited their woodpecker associations. Jupiter and Silvanus, the latter the god of forests, followed their Greek predecessors Zeus and Pan, respectively; Mars, like Ares, was the god of war, but he was also the god of agriculture and the woodpecker was allied to him in both roles. Ovid called the woodpecker 'the bird of Mars', and Plutarch wrote 'esteemed holy to the god Mars; the woodpecker the Latins still especially worship and honour'.[8] Plutarch also sought to explain this reverence when he stated:

Harking back to the legend of Picus, woodpeckers are popular logos in central Italy.

> For it is a courageous and spirited bird and has a bill so strong that it can overturn oaks by pecking them until it has reached the inmost part of the tree . . . [9]

Green woodpecker, cult bird of the Picenes and later the Romans.

69

Statue of Mars, the god of war, agriculture and woodpeckers, end of 1st century AD, from the Forum Transitorium, Rome.

Some claimed that Mars was also the father of Romulus and Remus, who as we recall were fed by a woodpecker, which is yet another link to the bird. References to woodpeckers can also be found in the writings of Horace, Virgil, Pliny the Elder and others. No wonder then that when the Roman legions marching into battle heard the woodpecker call or drum, it was hailed as a portent of victory. Interestingly, in his third-century *Deipnosophistae*, a monumental work which might be translated as 'Philosophers at Dinner', Athenaeus of Naucratis had listed woodpeckers among the delicacies of Greek cuisine.[10] The Romans, on the other hand, apparently refrained from eating its flesh as a mark of respect to the bird.[11] The mysterious, multifaceted figure of

Picus the woodpecker occurs in numerous guises in Roman mythology. He is variously the first king of Latium, a woodland king and a minor rural deity. He is described as the bird of Mars, even the son of Mars, or at least as a close disciple who was sacred to the god. Some believed he was the woodpecker that nourished Romulus and Remus, as described above. Picus also surfaces as an earlier version of Zeus, while in other accounts the two are rivals. In Virgil's epic poem the *Aeneid*, he is the handsome son of Saturn, father of Faunus and grandfather of Latinus.[12] In one celebrated legend the woodpecker was originally a man called Picus, the king of Ausonia and founder of Alba Longa, who, while on a hunting trip dressed in a fine red coat with a golden collar, was seen by the sorceress Circe, who fell in love with him. Using her magical powers, she separated Picus from his companions and declared her love for him. When Picus rejected her advances, preferring to remain faithful to his wife, Canens, the enraged Circe transformed him into a woodpecker with the same colours

Luca Giordano,
Picus and Circe,
c. 1655–60,
oil on canvas.

71

in its plumage as the man had had in his clothes (we might note that the red coat does not fit with the main plumage of any wood-pecker in Italy).[13] This fable is reproduced in Benvenuto Tisi's *Pico trasformato in Picchio*, painted between 1530 and 1540. The half-man, half-bird figure of Picus can be seen in the top right corner of this work, which today hangs in the Palazzo Barberini in Rome.

Picus is also credited with a talent for changing form and for augury, the practice of reading the will of the gods by observing the sky for signs, and was believed to have had such powers both before and after Circe changed him into a woodpecker. Ornitho-mancy (divination based on watching bird behaviour) was popular in Rome and it was assumed, for example, that the out-come of events could be deduced from observing the direction of a woodpecker's flight. In augury two categories of birds were considered, flying birds and calling birds, and woodpeckers belonged to both. In one particularly fanciful legend a wood-pecker once settled on the head of Aelius Tubero, the city praetor, while he was passing judgement in the forum. The bird was caught and the unusual event was interpreted by the augurs. They subsequently professed that Rome would be in danger if the bird was released, but that disaster awaited the praetor if the revered woodpecker was harmed. Aelius Tubero did his duty and promptly dispatched the unfortunate woodpecker; the perceived threat to the empire was averted, but, as foretold, the loyal prae-tor later came to a grim end himself.[14] In the forests of the Apennine Mountains in central Italy the Aequi people presided over an ancient oracle of Mars, and the prophecies there were supposedly articulated by a 'heaven-sent bird', presumably a woodpecker, also sometimes said to be Picus, perched on a wooden column.[15] In yet another version, Picus is a demigod who dwells outside Rome on Aventine Hill, where he spends most of his time in the company of Faunus, a demigod of nature, in a

John Gould, *'Gecinus viridis*: Green Woodpecker, or Yaffle', c. 1862, hand-coloured lithograph from *The Birds of Great Britain* (1862). Note the female has her long tongue extended.

dense, dark oak grove. Whoever and whatever he was, the multi-faceted Picus subsequently lent his name to the modern woodpecker-related ornithological terms of *Piciformes*, *Picidae*, *Picinae* and *Picus*. In most Graeco-Roman myths, however, the precise identity of the woodpecker species involved is unclear, although green ones occur repeatedly. Indeed, the bird we today call the Eurasian green woodpecker is widespread in Italy, but in some myths, particularly those referring to drumming, the black woodpecker, or even smaller woodpeckers such as the great spotted, may be the species the tales refer to.

The Americas are rich in woodpeckers, so it is unsurprising that they feature in the mythologies of indigenous peoples, from Alaska to Tierra del Fuego. These cultures had a very different relationship with woodpeckers from that of the European settlers who arrived later. The Europeans were monotheists and the former usually animists, with all wildlife part of their spiritual world, but this does not mean that woodpeckers were not killed – in fact we shall see that they were put to many uses, such as emblems and ornaments, as well as in medicines and rituals. Items found at archaeological sites in North America testify to the historical significance of woodpeckers to native peoples. A pre-Columbian seashell gorget unearthed at the Cox Mound in Tennessee (now in the Smithsonian) is engraved with four crested woodpecker heads. Crested woodpecker images also embellish ornaments of the Calusa tribe of Florida,[16] and pots from the Moundville site in Alabama.[17] Conch shells and axe handles with woodpecker motifs have also been found at the Spiro Mounds in Oklahoma.[18] Woodpeckers were particularly important to the cultures of the Pacific Northwest and Alaska, including the Karuk, Yurok, Hupa, Tlingit, Tsimshian and Gitxsan. These peoples hunted woodpeckers for their feathers, heads, scalps, tongues and bills, which were used to adorn ceremonial pipes,

headdresses and amulets. The Tsimshian and Gitxsan also carved woodpeckers into their totem poles. In British Columbia, one Gitxsan clan carved a giant woodpecker into its poles. Known as the Wee-Get-Welku, legend has it that this woodpecker was kept by a woman and fed until it grew so huge as to be uncontrollable, hacking into everything wooden that it could find until it had to be killed. As a mark of respect for the bird's power, it was incorporated into the clan's crest.[19] A commanding example of this pole, with the woodpecker sitting above a group of children and an eagle, stands in the Museum of Anthropology in Vancouver, with replicas in Gitanyow and Thunderbird Park in Victoria.

Of the thirteen species found in North America's Pacific Northwest, it is the largest, the pileated woodpecker, that assumed mythical status. It was most prized for its red-feathered scalp, which was used on ceremonial regalia and even as currency.[20] The Karuk called the pileated woodpecker the 'dollar bird' because its scalp could be worth that amount.[21] In Oregon, wealthy men from the Luckiamute tribe wore headbands

Native American rattle with a woodpecker.

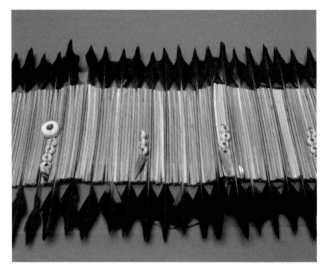

Native American headdress with flicker feathers.

Native American girl's dowry or puberty basket, late 19th century, with acorn woodpecker and other feathers.

Wee-Get-Welku woodpecker atop a totem pole.

Totem pole replica, with Wee-Get-Welku woodpecker at the top.

adorned with red woodpecker scalps to boast of their status. In California, some tribes performed rituals with dancers wearing belts made from northern flicker scalps.[22] In the Hupa tale 'The Scabby Young Man', a boy bravely obtains a blanket of scalps against all the odds, and hence rises in the esteem of his people.[23] The Hupa still have a deep spiritual relationship with woodpeckers, regarding them as messengers between the transcendent and earthly worlds. In their mythology, the spirit-being Kixunai has red hair and eyebrows, and the Hupa refer to red as the 'woodpecker colour'.[24] A Hupa and Karuk ceremony called the Woodpecker Hat Dance or Jump Dance invokes world renewal, a

John J. Audubon, 'Red-headed Woodpecker', from *The Birds of America* (1840).

key element in the belief systems of the region's tribes. Men dance, wearing headbands decorated with red woodpecker scalps, and chant solemnly, nodding their heads in the manner of woodpeckers pecking. In Idaho, the Kutenai also have a woodpecker ceremony, called 'Song to the Red-headed Woodpecker', where a shaman is awakened from a trance by the tapping of woodpeckers.

There are many references to a red-headed woodpecker in Native North American myths, but these do not necessarily mean the actual species of red-headed woodpecker; rather, in these stories it is any woodpecker with a red crest, crown or

The prized red crown and crest of a male pileated woodpecker, here on a living bird.

head. The woodpecker with the red head in the Lakota tale 'The First Flute', however, is likely to be the red-headed, as this species occurs across the Great Plains where the tribe lives. This woodpecker teaches a young man how to carve a flute from the branch of a cedar tree, and with it he successfully woos the chief's daughter.[25] Pawnee medicine men also wore headbands embellished with woodpecker scalps. For the Cherokee, woodpeckers were symbols of manhood and bravery; warriors carried the birds' heads with them into battle, the red crown symbolizing the bloodied head that awaited the enemy. Neighbouring Cherokee villages played a feisty ball game, before which they ritually painted and bled themselves; one player, called the *dalala*, the 'red-headed woodpecker', shouted aggressive challenges to the opposition.[26] The Caddo lived in the Piney Woods of eastern Texas. In their legend 'When Coyote Imitated His Host', Coyote meets Woodpecker, who has a light on his head. Coyote warns Woodpecker that he will catch fire, but the bird calmly tells him: 'I have always had this light on my head. It was given to me in the beginning. It will not burn anything.' Sometime later, Woodpecker visits Coyote and is surprised to see a pile of burning straw on Coyote's head. He warns him that he will catch fire, but Coyote tells him that he will not burn, as he too has always had a light on his head and at night he can do as he wishes, while others are in darkness. But just as he finishes speaking, Coyote's hair catches fire and he runs out of his lodge screaming for help. The message seems to be that the woodpecker's red head cannot be copied.[27]

The ivory-billed woodpecker was associated with leadership and warfare, and male birds, with their pointed red crest, were highly prized. John James Audubon wrote:

Travellers of all nations are also fond of possessing the upper part of the head and the bill of the male . . . the

80

strangers were very apt to pay a quarter of a dollar for two
or three heads of this Woodpecker. I have seen entire belts
of Indian chiefs closely ornamented with the tufts and
bills of this species.[28]

Archaeological finds suggest the importance of the bird's scalps,
which were used to adorn ceremonial pipes and regalia.[29] In the
eighteenth century, Mark Catesby remarked on the active trade
in its beaks, which fetched 'two or three deer hides a piece', and

were used to adorn 'coronets' made for distinguished hunters and warriors.[30] A bill found in a tomb in Colorado, well outside the historical range of the species, testifies to the fact that ivory-billed body parts were also prized in regions where the bird did not actually live.[31] Tribes as far north as Canada also traded for this bird with people from the southern United States.[32]

Interestingly, although woodpecker body parts have been used as totems and ornaments, unlike some animals woodpeckers have never offered much in the way of practical items that could be used in everyday life. However, the Seri people in the Sonoran Desert in Arizona and Mexico made use of one woodpecker product. The gilded flicker and the Gila woodpecker are two woodpeckers that are well adapted to this arid environment. Both excavate nest holes in the fleshy trunks and limbs of saguaro cactus, but the cactus treats these intrusive cavities as wounds and reacts by secreting a lignin sap that hardens around them, effectively producing a protective sealing shell. Remarkably, these woodpeckers do not attempt to use the holes until the following year, when the sap has dried fully and the scar tissue of the chamber wall is solid and watertight. When a cactus dies, its outer flesh rots away, but the tougher woody interior and the callus around any holes remain. These shells are angular in shape, keeping the form of the entrance and the chamber of the woodpecker nest, and are called saguaro boots. These boots can be found on the ground among the debris of dead cacti and were collected by the Seri and used as water vessels.

Clearly red, the colour of blood and fire, is significant, and numerous tales relate how woodpeckers acquired this colour. The fascination with red heads extended into Meso-America. In Mayan mythology, the earth goddess Chibirias painted the woodpecker's crest red with her brush. In another Mayan story, a woodpecker was asked to tap on a rock to find where it was

A saguaro boot, used as a water vessel by the Seri of the Sonoran desert.

thinnest so that man could extract the maize hidden within. The bird was cut by a sharp stone chip and bled, and the woodpecker has had red on its head ever since.[33] In Mexico, the red crest of the male imperial woodpecker was prized by native peoples.[34]

Imperial woodpecker pictograph, Casas Grandes, Chihuahua, Mexico.

The Anishinaabeg lived in the forested Great Lakes region of America. In their legend 'Manabozho and the Woodpecker', which occurs in several versions by other Algonquin tribes, the young Manabozho sets off to kill the nature-hating Spirit of Fever. Manabozho finds his enemy on a barren island with a single tree. A woodpecker sits on the tree and watches until the sun sets; when Manabozho gets tired, the woodpecker encourages him, telling him to aim for the top of his enemy's head. The warrior's final arrow goes straight into the spirit's top-knot, killing him.

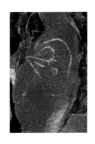

Manabozho dedicates his victory to the woodpecker by wiping his adversary's blood on its crown. Since then, woodpeckers have had red heads and have been objects of respect.[35] In their tale 'Little Grey Woodpecker', the Wyandot of Quebec relate how a small woodpecker got red on its head. The woodpecker would help a maiden paint her face, but on one occasion the girl left some rouge on her make-up brush. Because the woodpecker was plain grey with just a few white spots, he decided to try a little of the colour, rubbing some over both ears, and that is why today he has two tiny red marks on the sides of his head.[36] A curious thing here is the identity of the woodpecker described: no woodpecker in Quebec is grey, but the red marks on both sides of the head suggest, given the location, a male hairy woodpecker.

The Caribbean Taíno often painted themselves red, and believed that a sacred woodpecker had created women by pecking a hole into androgynous beings; since then all woodpeckers

The male hairy woodpecker, pictured here, appears in a Wyandot Nation tale.

have had blood-stained breasts.[37] The Embera of Panama and Colombia still believe that the woodpecker's erect red crest is a raised axe ready to strike, and the Huambisa of Amazonian Peru say that the woodpecker got its bright red head from the toucan in exchange for providing it with a nest hole.

In Europe, too, there are tales of how woodpeckers acquired red heads. In Bohemia the birds once voted the eagle to be their king, but the black woodpecker protested. Angered, the eagle pecked him on the head, drawing blood, and ever since, the woodpecker has had a red crown. In a Polish tale, God and the Devil were once friends, even working the land together. The Devil used horses to pull his plough, while God used a woodpecker, and thus the Devil got more work done. One night, God took the Devil's horses and finished his field. The next day the Devil was astonished to see this and, presuming that the woodpecker must be better at

The 'blood-stained breast' of a Puerto Rican woodpecker.

Crimson-bellied woodpecker, Peru. Woodpeckers with red heads were often revered by Native American peoples.

tilling than he had thought, asked to swap animals with God. The bird was, of course, hopeless, and in a rage the Devil struck it on its head, drawing blood which has remained to this day. In rural Austria woodpeckers were sometimes considered to be the Devil's herdsmen and shepherds, and the black woodpecker apparently got his red head, and the smaller ones their red 'bottoms', when their master beat them for not working hard enough.[38]

However, no matter how they got them, woodpeckers with red feathers are not universally considered to be positive birds. In Peru, the Andean flicker is locally called the lying flicker. Legend has it that the bird was sent by the Creator to announce to humans that fruit could be found both in the *puna* (the high treeless plain where this woodpecker lives) and down in the warm valleys, but the flicker mentioned only the valleys. As punishment for not telling the truth, the flicker bears a red wound on its nape.[39] In the Japanese tale 'The Sparrow and the Woodpecker', from Honshu, the woodpecker is a vain creature.[40] In this story the two birds of the title were once sisters. One day news came that their mother was dying, so the sparrow flew to her side, but the woodpecker took her time, standing in front of the mirror, putting on rouge, dressing up, and hence arrived too late. This is apparently why today sparrows, despite their drab plumage, live around people where they easily find food, while the woodpecker, despite having a prettier face, remains in the woods and has to work hard hammering at trees to find food. The woodpecker described is probably the Japanese woodpecker, which has a red stripe across both cheeks.

Woodpeckers often perch high on exposed snags, calling, preening and sunning themselves. Some tribes therefore linked woodpeckers to the sun, saying that their red crowns came from the light and fire above. The Secwepemc of British Columbia believed that the sun hatched from the egg of 'the rosy woodpecker', their name for the northern flicker.[41] Some alleged that woodpeckers stole or conquered fire. For the Sanpoil of Washington State, the woodpecker was 'the master of celestial and destructive fire'.[42] In their story 'Woodpecker and the Theft of Fire', the Sanpoil relate how long ago there were no people and there was no fire on earth. One day, the animal chief ordered everyone to go up and steal fire from the sky people. Every animal quickly made bows and arrows and began to shoot upwards to make a ladder, but the crafty woodpecker took his time, making a bow from the rib of an elk, arrows from the stalks of serviceberry (amelanchier) bushes, fletching from eagle feathers and arrowheads from hard flint. With these special arrows, the woodpecker was the only animal to hit the sky, making a chain that the animals climbed one by one. Once in the sky, everyone grabbed some fire and then rushed back to earth on the backs of the birds, with the sky people in hot pursuit. For some reason, Sapsucker was afraid to fly and so jumped instead, but hit the ground beak first; ever since, sapsuckers have had flat mouths and have to suck their food. Interestingly, in a myth of the Klikitat of the Pacific Northwest, Sapsucker is not so timid, and it is he who connects the earth to heaven with two parallel lines of arrows.[43] The Huichol of Mexico believe that they themselves created the sun. In their legend, a huge woodpecker, with the help of a squirrel, protects the newly forged sun from the arrows of the nocturnal animals. Both heroes are then killed for this act by the jaguar and the wolf, but to this day the woodpecker carries the colour of the sun on its bright red crest, and the Huichol offer sacrifices to it.[44]

Native Mexican Huichol shirt with woodpecker motifs.

The association of woodpeckers with fire is also found in the Old World. A woodpecker helps people obtain fire in the legend 'The First Fire', from the Congo. The bird pecks holes in the sky, which become stars, and, after assistance from a similarly helpful spider, a brave girl crawls through one of the stars and collects the fire beyond in a pot.[45] The Semang of the Malay Peninsula say the woodpecker is a sacred bird that should never be harmed, as it was the first to bring them fire, after stealing it from a stag.[46] Although no specific species are mentioned, it is likely, given what we know of associations between woodpeckers and fire elsewhere, that these woodpeckers had red on their heads. Red is time and time again the significant woodpecker colour for indigenous peoples worldwide.

Woodpeckers also occasionally feature in tales with another crucial element: water. The Biloxi people lived in what is now southern Mississippi and Alabama, and woodpeckers feature in their flood legend. They say that the waters rose so high that the birds clung by their claws to the clouds, but their tails dipped in the water. That is why the yellowhammer (flicker), the large red-headed woodpecker (probably pileated) and the ivory-billed woodpecker all have stubby tails. Actually, the tails of these wood-peckers are not particularly short, but perhaps they were perceived as such when compared to the many species of long-tailed birds. The Chitimacha of Louisiana say that the woodpecker (possibly a northern flicker) has a black tip to its tail because when the Great Flood arrived, it clung to a tree but its tail dangled in the dirty water. The Tlingit also associated the flicker with the flood, and a woodpecker features in the flood legend of the Cora in Mexico.[47] A tale from Alabama, 'How Water was Lost and Found', relates how a woodpecker ended a drought: after gambling away the family possessions, a man wagered and lost all the world's water. The wetlands dried up and people began to die of thirst.

Meanwhile *Bicici'hka*, a small speckled woodpecker with a red head, discovered a cane as big as a tree and began to peck it. Before he had made much of a hole, he heard a strange noise from inside and so flew away. After he was told that it might be water, he flew back and pecked a hole all the way through and water gushed out, quenching every creature's thirst. In another tale, by the Selk'nam people, who lived on the Tierra del Fuego islands in Patagonia, one of the folk heroes was the brave young Kákach, who fought Taita, a giant who was keeping people from drinking from the only lake. Kákach prepared for battle by rubbing his body with charcoal and painting his face red. After his victory everyone had water, but Kákach was no longer the same: he began climbing up and banging on trees and finally changed into a black woodpecker with a giggling call and red head – the iconic Magellanic woodpecker.[48]

Although many of the myths and tales involving woodpeckers are entertaining, some convey something deeper: an understanding among many indigenous peoples of what we now call ecology. The following two examples illustrate the point further. The Pawnee say that the woodpecker and the turkey once vied for the role of protector of people. The turkey laid many eggs and thus considered herself the perfect mother, as she cared for many chicks. The woodpecker believed she was better, as she made a safer home for her brood deep inside a tree. By the end of the year, most of the young turkeys had disappeared, but the woodpecker brood had all survived. Hence the woodpecker became the guardian of humans. This tale touches on the ecological reality that birds that raise their young in open nests lose more offspring than cavity nesters, and thus lay more eggs to compensate. Woodpeckers do indeed have a high brood survival rate.

The Lenapé of Delaware say that the sugar maple tree, infested by burrowing beetle larvae, asked the animals to rid him of the pests, but everyone was too busy to help:

So the maple asked the birds, but again most had no time to help him, except Papa'xes, the Woodpecker spirit, who also brought his cousins Ulikwán the Flicker and Titás the tiny Downy Woodpecker, to help rid Sugar Maple of the pests. It was hard work, but Sugar Maple was finally relieved and the woodpeckers happy with their insect meal. Many years later Papa'xes was in great distress, as it had not rained for many months and he was dying of thirst. So he went to Sugar Maple for help. Sugar Maple told the woodpecker to drill holes in his trunk and wait for them to fill with sap. So Papa'xes made many holes in Sugar Maple's trunk and sure enough the sap flowed and his thirst was quenched. Ever since woodpeckers have drilled holes and drunk sap from trees, and that is also how man learned that trees can be tapped for sap.[49]

Papa'xes is clearly a sapsucker, and this tale shows an insightful knowledge of the foraging and feeding methods of this bird. There may be a lesson for us all in this Kutenai creation story. Long ago the mammals and birds met and decided to create humans. The woodpecker, the flicker and the sapsucker were given the task of taking care of these new beings, and to ensure that they had a suitable environment in which to live and support themselves.

5 The Magic Woodpecker

The symbolism attached to the woodpecker occasionally seems uncertain and the bird has sometimes been linked to rather abstract themes such as good versus evil, black versus white magic, weather prediction and healing. In several cultures, ancient and more recent, woodpeckers have been associated with the elements. In particular, their drumming has frequently been allied with thunder and interpreted as the proclamation of a coming storm. In Mexico the Ixcatlan Mixe people called the imperial woodpecker Thunder's Chicken and said that it announced forthcoming rain,[1] while the Tzeltal Mayans associated woodpeckers with lightning.[2] In the Old World, in pagan Slavic mythology (particularly of the Croats), Perun and his wife Perunika were deities of thunder and lightning and in some accounts she prophesied storms and was associated with woodpeckers. In another southern Slavic legend, Vilas were alluring nymph-like feminine spirits who dwelled in wooded hills and mountain forests. Their cries were said to resemble those of woodpeckers and warned of impending tempests and other natural catastrophes.[3] In Norse mythology the black woodpecker was a bird of thunder and thus of Thor, while continental Teutonic tribes associated it with their thunder and war god Donar.[4] Some scholars of classic Greek mythology say that the Cretans worshipped a woodpecker before they did Zeus, the god of all Olympians whose main weapon was the thunderbolt, that is, lightning. He has also been variously described as the god of the sky, storms, wind and rain, and is credited with being able to influence them. In some accounts Zeus simply displaces the woodpecker as the idol but in others he seems to assimilate the bird and its abilities in a celestial personification and it has also been suggested that he in fact was the woodpecker.[5] Who and whatever Zeus was, his association with thunder and powers over the weather naturally allied him with the woodpecker.

Through its drumming the woodpecker has long been associated with thunder, but it is rain, perhaps more than any other climatic event, that has also been repeatedly aligned with the bird in lore. In ancient Rome it was a *pluviae aves*, a rain bird. Its alleged divinatory powers meant it could warn of bad weather, a skill highly valued by both military and agrarian planners; an avian weather forecaster no less! This belief continued through the ages and spread north across Europe, where there was the belief that the calls or drumming of a woodpecker foretold an impending downpour. As far as woodpeckers go the archetypical European rainbird was the green woodpecker, with the majority of tales and folk sayings on the subject involving this species.

In many European countries two *Picus* species, green and grey-headed, co-occur; as they are quite similar most people would not have differentiated between them and it is likely that the rainbird relates to both. If the drumming of a green woodpecker is mentioned as a precursor to rain, however, it is almost certainly the grey-headed that is being referred to, as, unlike its close relative, it drums fairly often. In countries where the green woodpecker does not occur, woodpecker weather lore refers to other species – in Finland, for example, the great spotted woodpecker takes up the role.

Woodpecker calls have been interpreted in different ways in relation to the weather in different countries and even between

Woodpecker weathervane, Dorset, England.

different regions within countries. In Austria, for example, a calling wryneck indicated rain, but in Estonia the same bird promised dry weather. The time or season that a woodpecker called in was also often significant, as this petite ditty from France illustrates: 'Si en juillet le pivert crie, il annnonce la pluie' (If the green woodpecker calls in July, it is announcing rain).[6] In Estonia hearing any woodpecker, but particularly a black woodpecker, calling in summer meant rain was on its way. Similarly, in Sweden hearing the call of a green woodpecker in summer was a sign of rain, whereas in winter it meant mild weather was coming.[7] Sometimes the prevailing weather influenced the interpretation and in Finland the great spotted woodpecker was regarded as both a bird of fair and foul weather: if one was seen on a rainy day that meant the weather would soon clear up, but seeing one on a sunny day meant it would soon rain. All in all, it seems the woodpecker, in common with some modern human weather forecasters, had everything covered.

The following tale from France seeks to explain from a Christian creationist perspective how the woodpecker became

The Woodpecker pub, Dorset, England; in some folktales woodpeckers are said to be always thirsty.

The Woodpecker pub, Berkshire, England; another thirsty woodpecker.

the rainbird. When God created the world he wished to provide rivers, streams and springs, so he asked all the birds with strong bills to help dig them. Only the lazy green woodpecker refused, but was punished for this, doomed never to drink from these water sources. For this reason, when the woodpecker is thirsty it is forced to look heavenwards and beg with repeated calls for rain to fall on branches and leaves, the only places from where it can get water. As is often the case with such tales, slightly different regional versions exist. In one the woodpecker was punished by being doomed to forever peck into wood and drink only from raindrops, and that is why to this day it has to call for rain to fall. Another version ends with the statement that since that time it has been reluctant to get its feet wet in puddles and ponds and that is why it is often thirsty. Elsewhere in Europe, rather than

Even people who have never seen the actual bird might recognize the green woodpecker from this famous beverage.

Le Tapeur, the local Creole name for the Guadeloupe woodpecker.

ordering the birds to create wetlands, God demanded that the birds bring one dewdrop each from the heavens and drop them in special places, where the ocean and lakes would rise. Other tales place these events after the Flood when the earth was parched and the birds' task was to replenish it with water. Some people even believed that when it tapped on a tree it was simply because it was thirsty, but it also indicated that rain was on the way. Strangely, this belief also existed on the Caribbean island of Guadeloupe, although it is likely that it was imported there by French settlers.

It is usually futile to try to fathom the reasoning behind such tales, as it is generally lost (if it ever existed) in the mythological mists of time. Several things in the above tales, however, are peculiar. First, of all the European woodpeckers, the one that is best suited to dig into the ground is the green woodpecker, as it regularly does so when foraging with its large bill. So quite why it is singled out as the reluctant worker is unclear, although, as we heard earlier, European Christianity often portrayed the

Contrary to
an old myth,
woodpeckers do
drink from pools
and ponds.

woodpecker in a negative light. Second, in many other folk tales the woodpecker appears as diligent and hard-working, quite unlike the lazy bird described here. Third, I can reveal that woodpeckers have subsequently defied God's command that they should never drink from wetlands, as they most definitely do.

The notion of the woodpecker as a rainbird is also revealed in the rich variety of folk names that they have acquired across Europe. Some of these names were used very locally, differing from county to county. In England the green woodpecker was variously known as the rain-bird, rain-fowl, wet-bird, weather-hatcher, weather-cock and storm-cock, as when it called rain was said to follow. Other old English folk names for the bird, such as yaffin-gale, yappingale, yuckle, yockle, yaffler and yaffle (the last two still sometimes used) are based on onomatopoeic syllables imitating its laughing and chuckling cry, but the sound was nevertheless still said to herald rain.[8] In Wales, too, hearing the woodpecker's laughing call was regarded as a sign of coming rain or a storm. Local Welsh names such as *Caseg y drycin* (Storm Mare) testify to this.[9]

In parts of France the green woodpecker is still known as *pleu-pleu* (rain-rain). This is doubly interesting as the name alludes to the bird's association with the weather as well as its call. *Pleu-pleu*, however, more accurately recalls the call of the other 'green' woodpecker, the grey-headed, a species not uncommon in parts of France. In German-speaking areas of Europe there are many folk names linked to woodpeckers and rain, but they are used for just about any species and often differ regionally. The names *Giesser* (pourer) and *Giessvogel* (pouring bird) occur commonly, but in Switzerland they refer to the black woodpecker, in other regions the green woodpecker, and in Austria sometimes the wry-neck.[10] *Schniavogel* (snowing bird) appears and *Göösvogel* occurs in Styria, but all are associated, in the end, with the coming of rain. In the Tyrol and Carinthia the wryneck may be the *Regenbitter* (rain-begging bird) and in slang the *Pipivogel*, but the use of words like *gaiss*, *geiss* and *geiss* may also be transliterations of the call of the wryneck. Old folk names in Czech for the green woodpecker such as *díšt'ák'* and *dýšt'ák'* are associated with *déšt'* (rain) and also indicate a 'rain bird'.[11]

In some beliefs woodpeckers go beyond forecasting rain to actually being able to summon it to fall. Of course rainwater was, and is, crucial to all life and any animal that could beckon it was to be respected, even venerated. In societies practising animism, evoking spirits was part of the shaman's role and when he beat his drum in rainmaking rituals he emulated the drumming woodpecker. Some peoples believed that the woodpecker actually first taught people how to drum in order to bring replenishing rains. Several North American tribes believed it drummed to encourage the thunder spirits to make it rain. These heavenly events, however, have not always been attached to woodpeckers in indigenous cultures. Thunderbirds (not necessarily the same as thunder spirits) were widespread in Native North American mythology, particularly among the Plains and Pacific Northwest tribes. They are described as enormous birds that caused storms and thunder claps, and sometimes lightning bolts, by flapping their wings. Different tribes had different traditions regarding the thunderbird but, somewhat surprisingly, none seem to be based upon a woodpecker.

Weather, the seasons and farming are inextricably linked. The folklore of rural areas and agrarian societies is naturally fecund with weather symbolism, and woodpeckers often feature in it, usually powerfully. In the Venito region of Italy, for example, a folk rhyme runs: 'Quando canta il pigozzo di Gennaio, Tieni a mano il pagliaio' (When the woodpecker sings in January, hold on to the hay, as the wind may blow it away).[12] In Bohemia it was said that if the green woodpecker called during the winter, then that season would be drawn out and the advent of spring delayed – farmers took note accordingly. The wryneck is Europe's only truly migratory woodpecker. Most spend the winter in sub-Saharan Africa and then return to Europe to breed each summer. Wrynecks were once, in more bucolic times, fairly common in the south of England and locally sometimes called the barley bird as their arrival usually coincided with the spring sowing of that crop.[13] A folk name for the wryneck in Switzerland also associates it with the promise of good weather, the repetitive call being interpreted as *Weib, Weib, Weib*, prompting people to say that winter was over and summer on its way as the bird was calling his wife.[14]

Yellowhammer (yellow-shafted flicker), state bird of Alabama, on a USA postage stamp.

Above all, it is the woodpecker's reputation as a rainbird, however, which has allied it to the fecundity and productivity of the soil. Across Europe farmers welcomed their calling and drumming as portents of the rain the crops needed. In rural France, when watermills were numerous, the green woodpecker was called *l'avocat, ou le procureur du meunier* (the miller's advocate, or lawyer). This was because the bird's calls were believed to attract rain, which besides quenching its thirst also filled the streams and powered the mills, much to the satisfaction of millers, who were always pleased to see the bird.

Like most woodpeckers, the flickers of the Americas are considered good omens, associated with friendship, family and good health. In a myth of the Alaskan Tlingit tribe, Raven told Flicker that he would be chief of all small birds.[15] In New England, the flicker was called the Shad Spirit, as it was said to prophesy the spring run of that fish.[16] Locally, and in tales, flickers are often called flickerbirds or yellowhammers. Alabama is known as the Yellowhammer State, a name dating from the Civil War, when a company of Confederate troops from Alabama arrived in Kentucky wearing uniforms trimmed with yellow. They were instantly

nicknamed yellowhammers, and the name stuck; Alabama veterans subsequently wore yellow feathers in their lapels and caps at reunions, and in 1927 the yellowhammer was adopted as the official state bird.[17]

Though woodpeckers are essentially arboreal, across the globe there are species that habitually search for food on the ground. The fittingly named ground woodpecker of southern Africa and the Andean flicker in South America are the most terrestrial, but many other flickers in the New World, several species of *Campethera* and *Dendropicos* in Africa and *Picus* in Eurasia, readily drop from the trees to probe turf and delve into soil for ground-dwelling prey. The bill of a typical arboreal woodpecker is straight and chisel-tipped, ideal for working on trees, but the more terrestrial species have a longer, decurved bill, perfect for prodding and digging into the ground. Metaphorically, it is a

The green woodpecker will probe into the ground in all weathers.

In some ancient mythologies the woodpecker's beak was seen as a plough. This is a streak-throated woodpecker digging into soil in India.

plough rather than a chisel. Such foraging behaviour and the ploughshare-like bill did not go unnoticed by ancient peoples and led to the woodpecker being associated with the fertility of the earth and used to symbolize tillers, sowers and cultivators, and it subsequently appears in legends and folk tales in these roles throughout history.

The so-called Fertile Crescent, which stretched from Egypt, the Levant and Mesopotamia to the Persian Gulf, is regarded as the birthplace of agriculture.[18] The biblical Garden of Eden itself is said to have been located there, in Mesopotamia, between the Euphrates and Tigris rivers. We have already heard how in that same region a sacred green-coloured woodpecker was associated with fertility. This bird was almost certainly what we now call the Eurasian green woodpecker as no other ground-feeding green species is found there. Interestingly, some taxonomists have proposed that the subspecies *Picus viridis innominatus*, which inhabits that area, be treated as a species in its own right, and given the name Mesopotamian woodpecker.[19]

The characters of Heavenly Ploughman and Heavenly Plough Animal, who pulled the first ploughs, are deeply rooted in the mythologies of ancient agrarian cultures. The woodpecker is often credited with having had this divine role and in many tales it even passes on the plough, and the expertise in using it, to mankind and oxen. The origin of the woodpecker and plough relationship is buried in the past, presumably deep in the Fertile Crescent, but seems to have been cultivated in Mesopotamia before moving on with wandering peoples and conquering and retreating armies to ancient Greece and Rome. Indeed, although the myth is pre-Hellenic we must look to Greece for explanations. Zeus, who as we have already heard had woodpecker connections going back to Crete, was also the lord of crops and the harvest in Athens. One of his many epithets was Zeus Georgos, god of crops and ploughing. Besides being known as the god of war, the Roman Mars, whose sacred bird was the woodpecker, was also originally a guardian of fields and crops. Ovid mentions that Triptolemos, the son of the green-coloured woodpecker Celeus, had a wooden plough and taught all of Greece the art of agriculture, but another account relates how it was Triptolemos together with his brother Jason who invented the plough before subduing and taming oxen and putting yokes on them. Some believed these 'Heavenly Twins', Triptolemos and Jason, were the offspring of Thunder and by association the woodpecker, the thunderbird.[20] In yet another interpretation it is suggested that Celeus himself did the ploughing.[21] Later, in Roman myth, it is the multifarious woodpecker deity Picus who fertilizes the soil. From Rome the concept subsequently took root in most of Europe: we might recall from the previous

Maroon
woodpecker,
known as Pangkas,
son-in-law of the
god Sengalang
Burong, among
the Iban of Borneo.

chapter how in a Polish tale God himself used a woodpecker to plough his field. Although the different interpretations of these mythical characters results in a rather muddled picture, the ploughing, weather and woodpecker associations and relationships were ever present.

Woodpeckers represent both good and bad in the mythology of the Iban of Borneo. They say the rufous piculet and maroon woodpecker are sons-in-laws of their god Sengalang Burong, and great importance is attached to their calls.[22] The piculet, called Ketupong, is the head of the seven omen birds in Iban culture and his calls are always heeded. The maroon woodpecker has two names, Pangkas and Kutok: the calls of the first can be either good or bad omens, but those of the second are always negative; for example, hearing Kutok call just as a battle begins is considered a bad sign. The symbolism attached to Pangkas is powerful but more convoluted, with much depending upon what one is doing when the woodpecker is heard. If it calls when a man is with a new wife for the first time, they should immediately separate and later renew their marriage vows. If a poor farmer hears it call while clearing trees for farmland, he will prosper, but if an already thriving farmer fells more trees, his success may wane. When Pangkas calls just as a hunting trip begins, it will be rewarding; if the call comes from the right during the hunt a large boar will be cornered by the dogs, but only killed after some have been wounded. A call when a warrior is making a wooden knife handle or spear shaft indicates that the weapon should be discarded, as it will later fatally wound its user, but if the weapon is inherited the portent is good and it will help him kill an enemy. If the woodpecker calls from the right as one leaves camp to go to war, another night should be spent at the camp, but hearing it to the right of the enemy camp is a good sign.

As in Borneo, the direction from which a woodpecker calls is also significant in Africa. In Kenya the Kamba tribe are wary of all small woodpeckers with red heads – several species there fit the description. They believe it is a good omen if one calls to the left of a traveller, but bad if one calls to the right. If it is heard up ahead then a lion or buffalo may attack. The Marakwet, also in Kenya, believe that all woodpeckers convey messages that must be heeded: seeing a Nubian woodpecker while on a journey

means it will be a safe and successful trip.[23] Presumably most of
the trips the Marakwet take are fruitful, as this woodpecker is
common and vocal in wooded savannah and easily encountered.
The direction from which the bird is sighted or heard is important
in Europe, too. Germanic tribes regarded a black woodpecker
flying on the left as a good omen whereas the Romans viewed this
as a bad sign.[24] Sometimes timing rather than direction matters.
Kārala is the folk name given to all woodpeckers in Sri Lanka, and
rural superstition there considers it unlucky for a person to hear
a woodpecker call when beginning a task or going to work, and
it is best to delay before starting again. If a *kārala* is heard before
an important meeting, it is advisable to postpone it.[25] In ancient
Greece, hearing a woodpecker call twice was a good sign, but
three times meant bad luck. If one was seen or heard on one's
right side it was a good omen, but if it appeared on the left, plots
against oneself were being incubated and hatched.

Sometimes, regardless of when, or from which direction they
called, woodpeckers just meant bad luck. In parts of Estonia the
wryneck's song was considered to bring misfortune and it was
generally believed that if a woodpecker with a red cap (several

John Gould, 'Black Woodpeckers', from *The Birds of Europe*, vol. III (1837).

species occur) was seen on a roof, there would be a fire, an accident or a farm animal would get loose. The black woodpecker has numerous folk names in Estonia, many referring to its black plumage. One particularly intriguing name is *jämaja*, which translates as 'bachelor's soul' and relates to young, frustrated, unmarried men who were considered to have a 'black soul'.[26]

Wrynecks can, as their name suggests, twist their neck awry. They do this when threatened or handled, but often just sway their head from side to side. The movement has been likened to a writhing snake, and in parts of Europe it is still said that wrynecks will hiss at the same time, seemingly imitating a serpent in an attempt to deter predators. In rural Austria, for example, wrynecks are known as *Aderwindl* (wriggling adder) and *Natterwindl* (also wriggling adder), *Natterfink* (adder finch) and *Natterzunge* (adder tongue). Actually, despite this idea being often repeated, there is no firm evidence that wrynecks intentionally imitate snakes in defence or attack mode, but nevertheless, this neck-twisting habit has resulted in their association with serpents in folklore across Europe, and by implication with witchcraft and the Devil. The pejorative image of the bird continued in recent times in Germany, soon after reunification, when people with rather flexible political positions became known as *Wendehals* (wrynecks).[27]

The much misunderstood wryneck is not alone in being regarded as a wicked woodpecker. Selfishness lies at the heart of a woodpecker-related folk tale from Central and Northern Europe. The story of 'Gertrude's Bird' or 'Gertrude's Fowl' is found in several versions in Scandinavia, the Baltic States and Central Europe.[28] The basic narrative concerns an old woman who is turned into a woodpecker because she refuses to give food and water to a traveller. She is then, as the woodpecker, destined to forever seek her food by boring into trees and drinking only rainwater. Quite how this metamorphosis comes about, however, differs regionally. In Norway Gertrude is a grumpy, red-haired, elderly woman who wears a black dress and a white apron. She bakes wonderful cakes and places them on the window ledge to cool, but never shares them, warning off anyone who sees or smells them by tapping loudly with her utensils on the window or banging on her baking tray. She is turned into a woodpecker with a red head and black-and-white plumage by a mysterious old man who is refused a cake and rudely chided. Gertrude's tapping is now that of the woodpecker when it searches for food. In other versions the old lady bakes bread rather than cakes and also refuses to give water to thirsty travellers. She has a red cap or headscarf rather than hair, and an all-black frock. In others still, she acquires her black plumage from soot when she flies up the chimney after being transformed. In some accounts the tale has evolved from its earlier pagan roots and acquired a Christian theme: Jesus Christ, sometimes in the company of St Peter, is the one who is refused food and drink and who thus transforms the old lady. Gertrude is sometimes an ill-tempered shrew who makes her husband's life a misery, so much so that he swears he would rather go to hell than heaven if that means avoiding her after death. In this version she insults a poor traveller, threatens him with her broom and refuses him water. The traveller in question is Jesus and as Gertrude has ignored the gospel and not given a stranger water, she is transformed into a woodpecker, cursed to forever wander the forest with a terrible thirst and forever beg for rain with plaintive calls. Presumably the husband was satisfied. Interestingly, the woodpecker in this version is often green rather than black, and the myth of the woodpecker as a rainbird is incorporated into the story. Indeed, in most versions of the tale Gertrude's bird is clearly a black woodpecker, although the description from Norway suggests one of the pied species, such as the great spotted woodpecker, and in Wales and Scotland the green woodpecker replaces the black, since the latter has never occurred in Britain.

Another old woman who is transformed into a woodpecker is the main character in the Romanian folk tale 'The First Wood-pecker'. The woman, who was always poking her nose into other people's business, met a strange old man who offered her gold if she would carry a mysterious green bag to the shore and throw it into the sea. She readily agreed, but once she was out of sight deep in the forest she opened the bag, whereupon all the world's insects crawled and flew out. The woman tried to catch the insects and return them to the bag, but her arms began to turn into wings, her black dress into black feathers, her red headscarf into red feathers and her nose became a long, sharp beak. The woman became the first black woodpecker and to this day all woodpeckers follow her in searching cracks and crevices to gather up insects.[29]

A particularly malevolent woodpecker features in the Lithuanian tale 'How a Woodpecker Felled a Spruce-tree'.[30] Here an unspecified species alights on the top of a tree, confidently rocks back and forth and declares threateningly: 'I will chop this spruce-tree down, Make a cudgel of its crown, wave it once and at a blow, every beast I see lay low!' Rabbit heard him first and was terrified, then Wolf, Fox, Boar and even Bear feared the woodpecker would carry out his threat. They implored it to spare the spruce, but the woodpecker just repeated its rant. All five animals gripped the tree and vowed that it would not fall, but the woodpecker set to work and the spruce crashed to the ground. The animals begged the bird to stop, but it flew to another tree and cried 'Think before you make me frown, I have chopped the spruce-tree down!' to which Bear bemoaned 'And I thought I was holding it ever so tightly. Oh, that woodpecker, I've never met anyone as strong as he!' Quite what the moral of this tale is, if any, is uncertain, but clearly any creature that can outwit a fox and scare a wolf and bear is one to be respected.

In Cameroon, the woodpecker is portrayed negatively by the Bakweri. In one of their stories the woodpecker and the weaver bird begin as friends but end as enemies. One day the two birds went on a walk together, but when they realized they would not reach their destination that day, the woodpecker suggested they build shelters for the night. The weaver wove a nest and tied it to the branch of a coconut palm and the woodpecker made a hole in a nearby trunk. During the night a terrible storm raged and destroyed the weaver's nest and so, barely alive, he begged his companion to let him into his tree hole, but the woodpecker refused, angrily slamming the door on the weaver. Ever since the weaver and the woodpecker have been bitter enemies.[31]

The calls of woodpeckers have also been associated with death. On Guadeloupe in the Lesser Antilles it is said that when one taps on a tree someone close is going to die. The only woodpecker on the island, the Guadeloupe woodpecker, is mostly black and herein probably lies the negative connotation. In some areas of Sri Lanka, the harsh flight call of a flameback is also believed to foretell the death of a relative, and in Finland if the black woodpecker knocked on the wall or window of one's house a relative or friend would pass away. Similarly in Estonia if any woodpecker tapped on a house, or even called or drummed nearby, it was to

The mostly black plumage of the Guadeloupe woodpecker probably led to its association with death.

In German folklore, the burning of woodchips taken from below a black woodpecker nest meant good luck.

be scared off, but if it returned then a death was sure to follow. The woodpecker has also sometimes been portrayed as the *Todtenvogel*, the mythical German 'Death-bird'.[32]

Despite this association with death, in some areas of Germany the burning of woodchips collected from below a black wood-pecker nest in the hearth was said to bring good luck, and merely holding one of its feathers by the hearth was believed to bring luck in love.[33] In other parts of Europe, it is said that if a wood-pecker is the first bird seen by a girl on Valentine's Day, she will

not find a partner. The fact that woodpeckers raise their young in a sheltered nesting chamber has often led to them being symbolized as hard-working parents, good homemakers and associated with family values such as protection, dependability and fidelity. These values have sometimes coupled them with fertility, such as in forested Bohemia where woodpeckers are still traditionally associated with marriage.[34] In the Slavic mythology of the Balkans, the goddess of marriage and motherhood was Perunka, another woodpecker-connected deity, before Christianity arrived and redefined her as an immoral hag.

Lewis's woodpecker and chick at the nest in Oregon. Many Native Americans regard woodpeckers as good parents.

On the subject of Christianity, the bestiaries were works of medieval European parables that used animals, both real and mythical, to teach moral lessons. In contrast to most of the pagan fables that came before, these Christian books of beasts rarely found a good thing to say about woodpeckers. Woodpeckers were

seen as heretics, their probing into trees interpreted as a search for evil in the hearts of everyone and the damage they inflicted upon trees likened to the sin with which Satan weakened the soul. This flawed notion, that woodpeckers destroyed trees rather than the insect pests they sought, illustrates the lack of understanding of the natural world which was so typical of that era, and can be contrasted to pagan beliefs that mostly got it right. Indeed, this negative viewpoint is in sharp contrast to how the bird was regarded in animistic societies. However, the symbolism of the woodpecker in European Christianity was inconsistent. The bird was occasionally perceived as good, that same tenacious probing and pecking sometimes equated with unremitting prayer, and the relentless quest for grubs within trees signified the rooting out of evil. Woodpeckers are not mentioned in the Bible, therefore most interpretations in the bestiaries probably derived from the likes of Pliny the Elder, although not from Aesop's Fables as woodpeckers are surprisingly absent there, too.

The *Jataka* tales from India centre on the previous animal incarnations of the Buddha.[35] In 'The Woodpecker and the Lion'

Northern flicker feeding its nestlings. Woodpeckers create safe and cosy homes in which to raise their young.

Detail from the 'Beatus' page of the 13th-century *Alphonso Psalter*, showing a green woodpecker and a kingfisher.

the Buddha appears as a shrewd but wary woodpecker who helps the lion but receives no thanks. In 'The Woodpecker, Turtle and Deer' the quick-thinking woodpecker saves the lives of its two friends from a hunter. Woodpeckers also appear in the *Panchatantra*, a collection of Sanskrit animal fables believed to be from the third century AD. In 'The Duel between Elephant and Sparrow', a woodpecker joins a frog and a gnat to get revenge on an elephant that had killed the chicks of their friend the sparrow.[36] Another wily yet helpful woodpecker is the main protagonist in a tale from the reindeer-herding Nenets people of Siberia. The woodpecker takes pity on two elderly wolverines, whose boat laden with all their belongings had been robbed by a fox. The fox is the cunning, sly animal typical of so many tales, but the woodpecker outwits him, using his bill to drill holes in the boat and forcing the fox to swim to shore before blocking up the holes and rowing back to the wolverines. To show their gratitude the female wolverine makes clothes and embroiders a black-and-white hat for the woodpecker and the male gives him a strong bill and sharp claws. The woodpecker has, ever since, had fine pied clothing tools to help him find food and lives high in trees out of reach of the fox.[37] This is of particular interest as it is one of the few tales involving a woodpecker which does not have red on its head. Given the location, and the description of its plumage, the woodpecker here can only be a Eurasian three-toed woodpecker. On the other hand, not all Russian woodpeckers are as smart as the one above. In Aleksandr Afanas'ev's celebrated collection of Russian folk tales, the woodpecker in 'The Fox and the Woodpecker' is easily tricked by a cunning fox. One by one, she drops her chicks down to him from the safety of their nest hole in an oak tree and, as we might expect, rather than teaching them a trade as promised, the fox eats them. In 'The Dog and the Woodpecker', however, the bird is not so naive. It befriends an old dog when its masters abandon it and is cunning and even vicious when confronted by peasant folk.[38] In most of these stories the message is that the woodpecker, though good-willed, is a character that should not be messed with as it will readily use its formidable bill as a weapon against much bigger foes.

The reverence that woodpeckers have received has stemmed mainly from the perception of their paranormal strength: after all, any bird that spends much of its life banging its head on hard tree trunks without falling down dead or bleeding from an injury, or at least suffering constant headaches, must surely be supernatural. To ancient cultures, woodpeckers seemed miraculous. Of course, today we know that woodpeckers are able to behave as they do because of their impressively evolved anatomy, but it should come as no surprise to learn that in the past people have put this all down to magic.

In Namibia the Owambo people believe that anyone who harms a baobab tree will be caught by its branches and swallowed whole; inside the huge trunk, victims wail and chant farewells to their families. Yet there is hope in the form of the woodpecker, who possesses the magic to open the mighty baobab with its bill; however, the bird may ask for payment, and may even refuse, as it is not always enamoured of humans who cut down trees without its permission.[39] High in the Andes of South America there is a bird that breaks the mould: a woodpecker that does not peck wood. The Andean flicker lives mostly above the treeline in the stony grassy terrain of the *puna* and *páramo*, where it forages on the ground, digging into soil and probing tussocks with its impressive bill. It even excavates its nesting cavity in earth banks and walls rather than in trees; indeed, there are not many trees to perch in or peck where it lives.[40] The indigenous peoples of the region believed that this terrestrial woodpecker carried a magical plant in its bill with which it could soften and split rock. In Peru the Incas are said to have acquired the secrets of this mysterious plant from watching the flicker at work and used this knowledge when constructing their impressive monuments.[41]

But it is in the Old World that the mythic relationship between the woodpecker and the magic plant is most prevalent – it has been suggested that the story arrived in the Andes with the colonizing Spanish in the sixteenth century and the Inca myth developed retrospectively. In fact, the folklore and superstition surrounding this fascinating plant and the woodpecker antedate the colonial Spanish. Its roots are planted firmly in ancient times. The Romans believed that the woodpecker watched over a magical herb which could cure disorders of the digestive system and of women's reproductive systems. Pliny the Elder mentions this in his *Natural History*, stating as his source the Greek Theophrastus some three hundred years earlier:

> There is a common belief that when wedges are driven into their holes by a shepherd, the birds, by applying a kind of grass, make them slip out again. Trebius states that if you drive a nail or wedge with as much force as you like into a tree in which a woodpecker has a nest, when the bird perches on it, it at once springs out again with a creak of the tree.[42]

It may go back even further, possibly originating in the Middle East in tales of similar mysterious, enchanted plants in the *Arabian Nights* and the Talmud. In Jewish myth, the shamir was a magic worm that could split and cut stone. In the story 'Solomon and the Demon King' a woodpecker appears as the avowed guardian of the worm.[43]

Clearly there has been a fascination with a magic plant through the ages, but what exactly is it? No one is certain. It can be found under the folk names of key-flower, wonder-flower, spring-wurzel, moonwort and, most frequently, springwort, but it has not been reliably identified as a known species. Several quite unrelated plants have been suggested, but the identity of the wondrous plant associated with the woodpecker remains shrouded in myth. The peony (there are several *Paeonia* species in Europe) regularly crops up as a candidate. This flower has been associated with fire in popular lore, as indeed has the woodpecker. Another link between this plant and the bird can be found courtesy of the Greek nature deity Pan, who has been allied to the peony and was said to have hatched from a woodpecker egg. The peony, particularly its root, has been used in Europe since ancient times to treat a variety of ailments and is still used by herbalists and traditional medical practitioners in the Far East. In Western medicine, several compounds have been obtained from the peony, including plant steroids – which might tempt some to add weight to the concept of the great strength often associated with the woodpecker. In his nineteenth-century treatise *Teutonic Mythology*, Jacob Grimm mentions both the peony and caper spurge (*Euphorbia lathyris*) as the possible 'explosive root'.[44] Other plants proposed include St John's Wort (*Hypericum perforatum*), maidenhair fern (*Adiantum capillus-veneris*) and Solomon's seal (*Polygonatum multiflorum*).

Variously described as grass, hay, flower, herb and root, the mysterious plant was credited with a range of magical properties. It was generally believed to bestow phenomenal strength on the woodpecker and on anyone else who could get their hands on it; rubbing it into the limbs or taking it as an invigorating herbal infusion was thought to confer superhuman strength. In France, it was said that one should never confront a man who had the plant in his pocket. It could purportedly soften iron and sharpen metals better than any grindstone; sickles and scythes whetted with it would cut like a razor. It also provided protection from metallic tools and weapons, and in some stories it opened locks. In Estonia the plant was obtained from the black woodpecker, and it was alleged that if held in the right hand between the thumb and index finger, all locks touched with it would spring open. It could unearth hidden treasure and allow access to usually impenetrable places. Sometimes such sealed places were symbolic: a suitor who had the plant could unlock the affections of an otherwise indifferent lady, as the woodpecker did its hole. The potent symbolism is clear, with the woodpecker's association with fertility alluded to. Some believed the plant to be medicinal, a cure for many ailments, but particularly those of the digestive system and those of women, soothing the pains of menstruation and childbirth.

The woodpecker, however, had a role in all this, and the plant could not be obtained without the bird. Some believed that it actually grew inside the bird's nest hole, but usually it was said to grow in secret locations that only the woodpecker knew. The bird had to be tricked into bringing it and giving it up. The most commonly quoted method was described by Pliny, and subsequently recounted by the Brothers Grimm in a version from German folkloric tradition. The ploy was to plug the hole of a woodpecker with a wooden bung when it contained nestlings. When it found that its chicks were imprisoned, one of the parents would fly away to get the plant. Upon its return it would perch with it in front of the nest entrance, and that would be enough for the bung to pop out of the hole. In other versions, the woodpecker touches the plant to whatever is blocking the hole, which then falls out. In any event, the bird then drops the plant on the ground, where it can be collected. The observation that the bird will bring the plant to unblock the hole only when it houses a brood of chicks is a realistic reflection of woodpecker behaviour, as most rarely bother to defend a clutch of threatened eggs.

As usual, there are variations of this myth. Some accounts indicate that after sealing the hole it was important to place a red rag or cloth on the ground below the tree. When the hole was opened and the woodpecker dropped the plant to the ground, it would not try to retrieve it because it was afraid of the colour red. Others said that the woodpecker would think a red cloth was a flame, and so would deliberately drop the plant onto it in an attempt to save the nest tree from burning down. In a seemingly contradictory account, a white cloth was sometimes recommended. Others believed that it was enough to simply shout and startle the woodpecker into dropping the plant when it arrived, rather than wait for it to unblock the hole.

In France, the green woodpecker was thought to obtain the strength to peck into hard oaks from occasionally rubbing and sharpening its bill against the plant. Green woodpeckers do habitually forage on the ground, probing into turf for ants with their bill or licking them up with their barbed and sticky tongues. Was such behaviour misinterpreted as the bird intentionally rubbing its bill against vegetation? Rather than trying to attract the bird by blocking its hole, another tactic was to find where the plant grew by covertly watching and following the woodpecker's movements. The bird, however, would always take care not to be followed, and the secret location was hard to find; hence in parts of rural France, the laughing call of the green woodpecker was said to be the bird mocking those wandering the countryside trying in vain to find its magic plant. There was also a belief that the woodpecker guarded the magic plant and would do so formidably. Anyone who sought the plant was advised to do so under the cover of darkness; otherwise, the bird would attack the intruder and try to poke his eyes out. Some said that one would go blind by merely seeing the woodpecker when attempting to collect the plant. Widespread in Central Europe, this belief can also be traced back to at least the Romans.[45]

Throughout the ages, magic has been invoked to maintain good health and to fend off death. The woodpecker's woodworking abilities led to it being bestowed with mysterious powers by the Romans. For example, the bill of the black woodpecker was alleged to have the strength of the gods and could thus fend off danger, and so it was carried as an amulet against stinging and blood-sucking insects. In twelfth-century Germany, the polymath Hildegard von Bingen described the green woodpecker as being the strongest of all woodpeckers, before adding that 'This bird's nature is clean, its heart simple and without any evil art.' Yet being so highly thought of did not spare the unfortunate bird – in fact, being regarded as pure was its downfall as parts of it became vital ingredients in some of Hildegard's medications: 'A person who is leprous should roast the green woodpecker on a fire and eat it often; it will destroy the leprosy.' Alternatively, an ointment made from the woodpecker's skin and flesh, mixed with vulture and deer fat, could be used to 'frequently anoint the person's leprosy and, no matter how strong the leprosy is, he will be healed'. A remedy for gout, clearly for the wealthy only, stated, 'dry the woodpecker's heart. Set it in gold and silver, as if it were a ring. When you carry it with you, *gicht* will go from you.' Hildegard also abruptly advised that 'Other parts of the woodpecker are not useful for medicine,' which was surely of great relief to the bird. Finally, despite meticulous preparation and administration of her concoctions, the pious lady declared that none would work 'if the judgement of God does not allow it'.[46]

Folk remedies, too, often involved killing and eating animals that were admired and respected in order to acquire some of their perceived magical qualities. Even in quite recent times, quack doctors have prescribed animal body parts to cure all kinds of complaints and disorders. Appallingly, the practise continues today in traditional Chinese medicine, with the rarity of the animal no deterrent. Just about every bird in the world has been regarded by someone somewhere as being of medicinal use, a dubious honour woodpeckers have not escaped. As we might expect, most of the recipes and remedies involving woodpeckers are weird and wonderful, though not necessarily for the poor birds themselves. We have already learned that Aiona, the god of the Ainu of Hokkaido, ritually killed and consumed the woodpecker after it had taught men how to carve canoes from logs. They also applied a woodpecker's feathered scalp to the head to relieve a headache, and spread the woodchips from its excavation work on painful boils.[47] Across the Sea of Okhotsk in Siberia, people used a woodpecker bill to soothe toothache, woodpecker eggs for tuberculosis, its blood for scrofula and powder from a mummified woodpecker for fevers.[48] Another Siberian people, the Tuaguses, used the pulverised flesh of the grey-headed woodpecker not as medicine but as a poison. Such was the potency of this concoction that arrow tips dipped in the powder were said to bring down any game they struck. In North America the Sac and Fox tribes believed that a desiccated woodpecker placed in a pouch would magically transfer the bird's ability to find hidden insect prey to the hunter, who could then find game.[49] On the subject of hunting, an old and somewhat bizarre belief in Estonia alleged that woodpecker blood was a wondrous lubricant for guns.

In Mexico, the Tarascan still place red woodpecker feathers in the hair of their children to ward off the evil eye and the illnesses it brings. The Tepehuán and Huichol used various parts of imperial woodpeckers to cure a range of ailments including earache, and mummified bodies discovered in caves there had the feathers of this woodpecker and other birds between their loins, presumably in the belief that they would magically preserve the corpse. Another Mexican people, the Tarahumara, apparently regarded nestling imperials as a delicacy.[50] The Bribri of Costa Rica and

Various parts of the Andean flicker have been used in Peruvian folk medicine.

Panama believed that gently stroking the body with woodpecker feathers could magically heal a sick person. In lowland Peru, the heart of any woodpecker mixed in wine and consumed was used to treat epilepsy, and up in the mountains the blood of the Andean flicker was mixed with wine and drunk to treat heart conditions and tuberculosis or used as ear drops to counter hearing loss caused by the chilly *puna* winds.

In Europe, too, specific woodpecker species were often required in folk remedies. In France, eating a green woodpecker complete with its feathers apparently protected the diner from black magic. In the Austrian Tyrol, the body of a grey-headed woodpecker placed under the pillow of a child was believed to prevent spasms, while the flesh of the green woodpecker was eaten to treat epilepsy. In Moravia, epileptics were allegedly cured by making the patients sit and literally smoke among the burning feathers of a black woodpecker. A little further north in Germany, a medieval formula recommended ground green woodpecker bones mixed with white wine as a remedy for kidney and bladder stones, while the litter from its nest hole (woodchips and droppings, as woodpeckers do not use nesting material proper) was placed on the head to banish a headache. In Bavaria and Austria a soup of woodpecker flesh and horseradish was drunk to treat lung infections and the gall of a wryneck was used to thin bushy eyebrows. Anyone bitten by a dog had only to partake of a few black woodpecker droppings to heal the wound. Quite why no other woodpecker species' droppings would do is unclear.[51]

For some Native North Americans, woodpeckers were medicine birds. Some California tribes believed that if a man dreamt of a yellowhammer (yellow-shafted flicker), he would become a healer. Shamans of the Nez Percé tribe believed that they could invoke the magic powers of the woodpecker during exorcisms. These tribal wise men sought to cleanse the possessed in the same way that a woodpecker extracts a grub from a tree. On the same theme, a tale from Vietnam relates how a proud oak tree only wanted songbirds like the lark to visit him and chided the ugly woodpecker for pecking noisily upon his trunk while he was resting. The woodpecker calmly told the tree that he was actually helping him by removing harmful grubs, but the oak just bragged that he did not need help as he was big and strong. Sometime later the oak began to feel unwell as the grubs grew and riddled him with their burrows, and when his leaves turned yellow and the pain increased, he pleaded with the songbirds to help him, but their bills were too small and weak to get at the pests. Then he remembered the woodpecker and begged him to return. The woodpecker carefully inspected the oak and pulled out the grubs before flying off to help other trees in the forest.[52] A similar notion is held in Central and Eastern Europe, where generations of Czech, Slovak, Polish and Hungarian children have learnt that woodpeckers are the doctors of trees. The woodpecker gently taps with its bill on trees and, just as a doctor taps a patient's chest during examination, it diagnoses trees made sick by insect pests and then operates, surgically pulling the grubs out. This belief is so deep-rooted that even those children who become

John J. Audubon, 'Golden-winged Woodpecker (Yellow-shafted Flicker)', from *The Birds of America* (1840).

In Costa Rica, the Bribri associate the pale-billed woodpecker with childbirth.

hunters and foresters in adulthood habitually maintain their respect for the woodpecker, the original tree surgeon, and understand the role it plays in the forest ecosystem. The truth, though, is that the woodpecker does not magically cure trees plagued with invertebrates: it simply dines upon the insects.

Woodpeckers also play a role in birth and fertility rites in several cultures. In a symbolic birth and creation myth, the Suruí, of Rondonia in Amazonian Brazil, relate how various forest birds tried to crack open a rock to release the people trapped inside, but all except the woodpecker broke their beaks doing so.[53] The Caribbean Taíno believed that the nesting cavity of the woodpecker (created by its 'magic beak') was a womb, and the emergence of young woodpeckers from it was associated with the birth of a child. The Bribri still believe that if a pale-billed woodpecker calls, a woman has become pregnant or a baby is soon to be born.[54] The Waiwai, who live in the Amazon rainforest in Guyana and adjacent Brazil, say that if a woodpecker calls *swis-sis*, a boy will be born, but if a woodpecker drums *tororororo*, the child will be a girl. In lowland Peru woodpecker feathers were said to prevent miscarriages and ensure the smooth delivery of babies.

Returning to the Andes, the ever unfortunate Andean flicker was also credited with being able to help nursing mothers and lactating livestock produce more milk. Once trapped and killed, its toasted flesh and feathers were ground up to be sprinkled in soup for new mothers; for consumption with animals, the woodpecker's ashes were mixed with meal, mint, fennel and salt. Pre-Columbian in origin, this belief apparently still lingers today in some remote areas. If all this was not enough, the tongue of the flicker was kept as a magic lucky-in-love charm.[55]

6 Woodpeckers Today and Tomorrow

So it seems that woodpeckers, in all their glorious diversity, have fascinated humankind throughout the ages. Woodpeckers are a complex subject, portrayed as both kind and cruel, clever and naive, harbingers of good or bad luck, and associated with life as well as death. These opposing representations, furthermore, can occur within individual cultures. But where do they sit in the modern world? Perhaps reflecting the USA's dominance in popular culture and news media, the three woodpeckers that have attracted the most attention in the modern era all hail from that country. Namely, the long-lost ivory-billed woodpecker, a northern flicker that gave NASA a headache and a rascally cartoon character.

In 2005 it was announced that the ivory-billed woodpecker, a bird with a historical range that covered the southeastern USA and Cuba but had not been seen with certainty since 1944, had been sighted in Arkansas in April 2004.[1] This news sparked a media sensation, even making the front page of the *New York Times*, but the main evidence presented – brief observations and a poor-quality video – did not convince everyone. The U.S. Fish and Wildlife Service, however, was convinced and a series of searches were made over the next five years. Nothing conclusive was found and few now believe that this woodpecker survives in the USA. Nevertheless, it is still officially classified as critically endangered rather than extinct.[2]

The arguments for and against the continued existence of the ivory-billed woodpecker, and whether it was rediscovered in 2004 or not, have been done to death. A surprising number of birders, ornithologists and writers seemed to take the rediscovery story, and the bird itself, to heart, with some seemingly staking a personal claim to it. The ivory-billed is one of the least

Male ivory-billed woodpecker in the Natural History Museum, Vienna.

photographed North American birds ever, yet it is probably the most written about. The debate has raged on for years with an intensity more typical of political or religious disputes. In the years following the 2005 announcement there was a deluge of scientific papers, birding articles, newspaper stories and internet posts devoted to the species. There are more books on the ivory-billed woodpecker than on any other wild species of this bird family, including *The Grail Bird* (2005) by Tim Gallagher (one of the rediscoverers), *Stalking the Ghost Bird* (2008) by Michael K. Steinberg and *Ghost Birds* (2010) by Stephen Lyn Bales. Phillip Hoose's *The Race to Save the Lord God Bird* (2004) had appeared before the Arkansas news broke.

The titles of these books – invoking grails, ghosts, god – are revealing, setting the debate in a religious or supernatural context. Chapter Sixteen of *The Grail Bird* is even titled 'The Lazarus Bird'. This story became both political and religious as the arguments about whether the bird had actually been resurrected or not assumed an almost religious fervour. Those who refuted the wood-pecker's existence were labelled nay-sayers and those who accepted it were, in their own words, believers; others declared themselves agnostics. An Ascension sermon given in Philadelphia soon after the rediscovery announcement comforted the congregation with the words 'if even the woodpecker can return, then maybe we humans aren't so impossible after all.' A Lutheran seminarian in Ohio found in the story 'a sign that humanity's sin . . . is not yet final or complete'.[3] A critic of the original paper on the rediscovery used the term 'faith-based ornithology' to describe what he believed was the triumph of hope over proper field observation.[4]

Not everyone was using religious terminology, however. 'Elvis' was the code name for the secret search for the woodpecker, and headlines pronounced 'Elvis Found' and 'Elvis in Feathers'. Although not a biblical reference, the use of the name Elvis certainly continued the trend of the need to believe in resurrection. Then again, in certain circles in the u.s., especially in the parts of the country where the woodpecker was rumoured to have survived, Elvis Presley is the subject of a cult that can be described only as religious; in other words, calling the bird Elvis was every bit as religious an act as calling each other heretics and faith scientists. So commanding was this woodpecker story that even the Republican administration of George W. Bush, not noted for its conservation policies, enacted protection measures. Since 2005 the ivory-billed woodpecker, dead or alive, has nestled into the cultural conscience of many in the u.s., morphing into a story about people rather than a bird, a tale of human hopes and dreams. It is highly unlikely that those for whom the ivory-billed woodpecker took on such significance will ever see the actual woodpecker, but just as Native North Americans had their spiritual woodpeckers, now modern America does, too.

Northern flicker on NASA space shuttle *Discovery* STS-70.

NASA space shuttle
Discovery STS-70
with woodpecker
holes repaired.

Ten years earlier, another woodpecker hit the headlines. Don
Thomas was an engineer and astronaut on the National Aero-
nautics and Space Administration (NASA) space shuttle *Discovery*
STS-70 project in the 1990s. In his book *Orbit of Discovery: The All
Ohio Space Shuttle Mission* (2014), Thomas relates how in 1995,
just over a week before the scheduled launch, it was noticed that
the foam insulation covering the shuttle's external fuel tank was
riddled with holes. The culprit was a male northern flicker (possibly two), which had bored more than two hundred holes into
the 7.6-cm- (3-inch-) thick material. NASA was forced to take the
shuttle back to the assembly building and repair the damage,
delaying the flight for a month. Owl decoys and balloons with
predator eyes were placed around the site to deter further attacks.
This is still remembered as 'The Woodpecker Mission' and 'The

135

Woodpecker Shuttle Flight'. In retirement, Thomas apparently does not hold any grudges against flickers; on the contrary, he respects them, even putting out food for them in his back garden.[5]

Probably the best known of all woodpeckers is not even a real bird. Woody Woodpecker is the only woodpecker that many people know. Woody appeared for the first time in 1940 in a cartoon entitled 'Knock Knock', which centred on the established character Andy Panda and his father being harassed by a wacky woodpecker with a crimson head and flamboyant crest. In his next cartoon, actually titled 'Woody Woodpecker', he was even wackier, visiting a psychiatrist fox who is driven mad himself by the woodpecker. Woody was apparently created when Walter Lantz was disturbed by an acorn woodpecker that continually bored holes into the California cottage where he and his wife were honeymooning. Lantz allegedly wanted to shoot the bird, but his wife suggested that rather than taking such drastic action he should use the woodpecker as inspiration for a new cartoon character. In 1947 the 'Woody Woodpecker Song' became a nationwide hit in the USA. Featuring Woody's mad laugh, it was even nominated for an Oscar for Best Song. In the late 1950s *The Woody Woodpecker Show* was successfully launched on television and Woody became an international icon, with a star on the Hollywood Walk of Fame. In Germany he was known as *Hacky der Specht*, in Italy *Picchiarello*, in Brazil *O Pica-Pau*, in Quebec *Woody le Pic* and in Spanish-speaking countries as *El Pájaro Loco*. His cartoons are still shown in many countries, although (like the ivory-billed woodpecker, to whom he has been compared) he is rarely seen today in his native habitat in the u.s.

Despite his fame, Woody was not an especially pleasant character; he was typically described as crazy, zany or screwball. His appeal probably lay in that very wackiness, mischievousness and outlandish plumage. The early Woody was a fairly crude, even

Woody Woodpecker, sporting very un-woodpecker-like blue plumage.

aggressive, character and eccentrically drawn with a huge bill and feet, goofy face with big eyes and technicolour blue and red plumage. In later versions he became less abrasive in both behaviour and appearance. Woody is clearly a woodpecker, but which one? We might ask, as Woody himself does in the famous opening line to his shows, 'Guess Who?' There is something distinctly American

about Woody, and of the 22 species present on that continent he is arguably, with his red crest and elongated physique, most like the pileated woodpecker. Then again, if the honeymoon story is true, Woody was based on an acorn woodpecker, and his famous manic, laughing call might suggest that species rather than the pileated. Regardless, the fact that Woody was mostly blue effectively eliminates all wild woodpeckers – though they come in many colours, no woodpecker on the planet is blue. Ultimately, of course, Woody Woodpecker is a stylized anthropomorphic figure, not a true representation of a wild species. Similarly, Woody's scripts owe little to real woodpecker behaviour (Lantz and his team were no ornithologists) and though Woody pecks and drums, many of his traits are decidedly un-woodpecker-like. Then again, in 'Termites from Mars' (1952), Woody's home is invaded by hungry intergalactic insects, a situation he resolves with adhesive tape; it is tempting to suggest that by using sticky tape Lantz was referring to the sticky tongue

138

that some woodpeckers use to catch prey. Later that year, in 'Scalp Treatment', the storyline alluded to the practice of some Native American tribes of using woodpecker scalps in rituals and as currency.

As we have seen, woodpeckers are often associated with a sound work ethic and reliability, an association that has proved popular in marketing. Along with these perceived positive values, the woodpecker image makes a striking logo, and has thus been incorporated into some emblems and coats of arms.

Woodpeckers have also appeared on postage stamps from Argentina to Zimbabwe, with countries as diverse as Bulgaria, Finland, Hungary, Malaysia, Mongolia and Vietnam releasing woodpecker stamp series. In 1978 North Korea issued five stamps highlighting their endangered white-bellied woodpecker, and in

Acorn woodpecker, allegedly the inspiration for Woody Woodpecker.

Town coat of arms,
Ganterschwil,
St Gallen,
Switzerland.

Town coat of arms,
Pielisjärvi, Finland.

Town coat of arms,
Sitke, Hungary.

2007 Serbia issued a series of four black woodpecker stamps in conjunction with the World Wide Fund for Nature. On 1 January 2000 the Central Bank of Suriname issued a five-gulden banknote with a red-necked woodpecker on the obverse.

It is probably safe to say that most people like woodpeckers. This may be because their fascinating behaviour and carpentry skills impress us, but it is also true that their perceived industriousness endears them to us. In the main, they are positively regarded and left unharmed, but those same woodworking talents can place them in direct conflict with people. As already mentioned, woodpeckers play a key role in the biodiversity of woodland ecosystems by creating cavities, but at the same time they are occasionally accused of damaging trees. The truth is that almost all the trees they choose to make holes in are already infected with diseases such as fungal heart-rot. Even though these trees may seem healthy from the outside, a closer inspection usually reveals that they were already rotten and doomed before the woodpecker set to work creating a cavity or searching for insect prey within. Some woodpeckers do damage utility poles and the walls and insulation boards of buildings by hacking holes in them, to the annoyance of utility companies and homeowners alike. The birds generally make more holes than they use, so such structures can become riddled with them. In the u.s., golden-fronted woodpeckers were taken off the protected species list for a time and culled because they bored into utility poles, and in the late nineteenth century a person was employed to keep red-headed woodpeckers off the wooden poles of the Kansas City tram system.[6]

So why do woodpeckers make holes in such non-natural structures? In some areas, it may be that a lack of natural sites is to blame after snags and dead trees have been removed. Perhaps it is simply that soft building timber and synthetic insulation are

easier to excavate than trees; despite their remarkable abilities and physique, woodpeckers often take the easier option. It has also been suggested that the high frequency sounds emitted by wires and electrical devices such as air-conditioning units and refrigerators may trick woodpeckers into thinking that invertebrates reside inside such structures. In some cases, it is simply because the building does indeed house invertebrates such as bees, ants or beetle larvae. Where they are protected by law, permits are issued to cull woodpeckers that cannot be deterred by other methods, but it need not come to that, as various means to discourage them can be employed instead. Woodpecker deterrents abound and include visual scares such as balloons, bird's

West Indian woodpecker pecking a utility pole in Cuba.

Utility pole riddled
with woodpecker
holes in the Czech
Republic.

eyes, raptor models and silhouettes, flash tape, netting, anti-woodpecker paint and non-toxic resin filler that discourages future visits by welcoming the arriving woodpecker with a bad taste and odour. Horticulturists, too, sometimes dislike wood-peckers for taking fruit, nuts and seeds. In the u.s., red-headed and Lewis's woodpeckers have a reputation for raiding orchards, and acorn woodpeckers eat cultivated pecans and almonds. In the Dominican Republic, a bounty was placed upon Hispaniolan woodpeckers when they pecked cacao pods for the nutritious pulp. Overall, any harm that woodpeckers do is negligible, prob-ably exaggerated and ultimately insignificant when compared to the damage humans inflict upon woodpeckers and their habitats. Thankfully, woodpeckers are nowadays increasingly regarded as beneficial rather than tree-destroying vermin. Research world-wide has shown that they are important natural controllers of forest insect pests. Examples include American and Eurasian three-toed woodpeckers, which regulate spruce bark beetle popu-lations,[7] and hairy and downy woodpeckers, which are important controllers of oak borer beetles.[8] On Indian coffee plantations,

Three-toed woodpeckers are natural forest-insect pest controllers.

rufous woodpeckers prey on the ants that nurture mealybugs, pests which are harmful to plants.[9]

The International Union for Conservation of Nature (IUCN) focuses on nature conservation and the sustainable use of natural resources. The IUCN maintains a Red List that classifies species depending on their global extinction risk. The highest levels of threat are critically endangered (CR), endangered (EN) and vulnerable (VU), which contain those species facing a very high risk of extinction.[10] As I write, eighteen woodpecker species are included in one of these three categories and, as most woodpeckers are arboreal, the main overall hazard is deforestation.

Most people today are probably aware of the ongoing degradation of the Amazon rainforest. What is happening in Brazil is disturbing, but the logging and burning of forests elsewhere on the planet is actually often worse when measured by the percentage of land-mass cleared. Here are just a few examples: Honduras in Central America was once almost totally forested, but today

Bark removed by three-toed woodpeckers searching for spruce bark-beetles in Slovakia.

Cut and burnt rainforest in Brazil.

only 50 per cent of that remains; it is thought that Haiti has lost more than 90 per cent of its original forest. Historically, about half of Nigeria was forested, but only around 10 per cent now remains. The Philippine islands used to be blanketed in forest, while now only 35 per cent is estimated to remain. Indonesia was also once almost totally forested, but around 35 per cent of that cover has disappeared, much of it in the past 25 years. Borneo is the world's third largest island, but logging activity there in recent decades has been astonishing, with more than half of the original lowland forest probably felled. Malaysia, too, has seen large areas of prime forest vanish.[11] Worldwide, besides commercial logging (legal and illegal), forests are also felled and burnt to create agricultural land. This depressing situation is disastrous for woodpeckers, as it is indeed for all wildlife, and for people.

South America is the world's woodpecker hotspot, but the natural history of many species, particularly in the Amazon basin, is poorly known. Kaempfer's woodpecker was rediscovered in

Remains of a woodpecker nest hole in a prematurely cut tree in Hungary.

Speckle-chested piculet, an endangered species of Peru.

central Brazil in 2006 after not having been seen for eighty years. Encouragingly, it seems to be on the increase, but is classed as endangered, as the *cerrados*-bamboo forests it needs are being converted to crops and plantations.[12] The varzea piculet is considered endangered as it is known only from a relatively small area in Amazonian Brazil, where deforestation is rife. In Peru, the speckle-chested piculet is also endangered as the forests it inhabits have been widely logged or converted to coffee plantations and pastures.[13] Fernandina's flicker, endemic to Cuba, is classed as vulnerable, with fewer than nine hundred individuals estimated to survive. Besides the cutting of its woodland habitat for timber and farmland, it suffers incidentally for having provided nest sites to the Cuban parrot (*Amazona leucocephala*). Poachers in search of young parrots for the pet trade fell trees with flicker cavities, and even when no parrots are found, the nest trees and any flicker clutches or broods are usually destroyed. Things cannot get much worse for the imperial woodpecker, which is listed as critically endangered, possibly extinct. It once ranged through the pine

Fernandina's flicker, an endemic, vulnerable woodpecker of Cuba.

forests of the Sierra Madre Occidental in Mexico, but widespread logging and hunting – for food, supposed medicinal properties, amulets and 'sport' – proved disastrous.[14] Up to 60 cm (24 in.) long, this largest known woodpecker species has not been recorded with certainty since 1956. There is a slim chance that a few imperials survive in areas that are currently inaccessible due to the activities of drug cartels.[15] Southeast Asia is another woodpecker-rich region. As already mentioned, the Philippines' forests have been heavily logged or cleared for farming, charcoal burning and development. The yellow-faced flameback and red-headed flameback are two endemics that are endangered. The former now occurs only on the islands of Negros and Panay, where most primary forests have been cut, and the latter on Balabac, Palawan and the Calamian islands, where the remaining lowland forests are fragmented. Another endemic, the vulnerable southern sooty woodpecker, is now scarce, and its habitat continues to be logged. The huge great slaty woodpecker is scattered from India through Indochina to Malaysia, Indonesia and the Philippines, but is classed as vulnerable, as the mature tall forests it needs have gradually dwindled. Found only in forest pockets in western Java, in areas where most lowland forest has disappeared, the tiny white-rumped woodpecker is also endangered. In eastern Java, the Javan flameback is classed as vulnerable and suffers from the same loss of forests to logging, mining and clearance for farming and construction.

Island endemics often exist in small populations that are very sensitive to change. The endemic woodpecker on the Japanese island of Okinawa was probably never very common, but is now one of the rarest woodpeckers on the planet. After first suffering from the logging of its forest habitat, the Okinawa woodpecker was then faced with dam, golf course and helipad construction for the U.S. Marine Corps, and threats from non-native predators

Male imperial woodpecker in the Natural History Museum, Vienna.

Most people seem to like woodpeckers.

such as feral cats.[16] Numbers have apparently stabilized recently, but the Okinawa woodpecker is still critically endangered.

There is relatively little data on the conservation status of woodpeckers in Africa. There are so many iconic mammals on the continent, some seriously endangered, that study and management efforts tend to focus upon those animals rather than woodpecker species. Stierling's woodpecker occurs as a fragmented population in parts of Tanzania, Mozambique and Malawi, where it is threatened by the clearance of its favoured *Brachystegia* woodland for firewood and tinder for drying tobacco.

There is only one species of woodpecker in Arabia, the aptly named Arabian woodpecker, which is restricted to the foothills above the Red Sea in Yemen and Saudi Arabia. It is uncommon and classed as vulnerable; once again, the cutting of trees is the main threat to woodpecker populations, as timber is collected for firewood and charcoal and woodland is cleared for farming and development.

Woodpeckers in North America and Europe are faring somewhat better. Although there are local issues for some, none of the eleven woodpeckers found in Europe are currently regarded as seriously threatened. In recent times, most woodpecker research and conservation measures were focused on three North American species: red-headed, red-cockaded and ivory-billed woodpeckers. The threats to these species are real (as already mentioned, the ivory-bill is probably lost), but unlike the case for many other, even more urgently imperilled, species, the fact that all three occur in the U.S. meant that funds were available to tackle the problems. Elsewhere in the world, research funding is harder to come by. Yet all is not lost; there are losers, but also winners in the woodpecker world. Those that have adapted to use man-made and urban habitats often thrive, and those that live in open woodlands can benefit from forest fragmentation.

Woodpeckers are some of the most magnificent birds inhabiting the planet's natural woodlands and forests. An English folk name of the green woodpecker is the yaffle, the laughing bird, and Woody Woodpecker, probably the best-known woodpecker ever, is also famous for his mocking laugh. Sadly, given the rate at which the earth's forests are being degraded and felled, we might ask whether the woodpecker will have the last laugh. There is hope, but the woodpecker is not out of the woods quite yet.

Timeline of the Woodpecker

25 MILLION BC	5 MILLION BC	3–5 MILLION BC	3000–1000 BC
Earliest fossil dated from this time, the late Oligocene epoch; found in France and named *Piculoides saulcetensis*	Woodpeckers as we know them today probably appeared around this time	Oldest African fossil dated from this time, the Pliocene epoch; named *Australopicus nelsonmandelai* after Nelson Mandela	Minoan mythology includes references to woodpeckers; early Cretans associate the bird with Zeus, father of the gods

c. 771 BC	mid-1ST CENTURY AD	AD 1000–1500	1498
Romulus and Remus are found and cared for by a she-wolf and a woodpecker	Pliny the Elder writes his *Natural History*, which includes some remarkably accurate descriptions of woodpeckers	Items from this period found at archaeological sites in North America are decorated with woodpecker motifs	Fray Ramón Pané compiles a study of the Taíno people and learns that they believe in a sacred woodpecker called *Inriri* that created women from asexual beings

1942	1955	1982	1995
James Tanner's *The Ivory-billed Woodpecker* is published in New York; it is the first monograph on a single woodpecker species	Heinz Sielmann's film *Woodpecker* (*Zimmerleute des Waldes*) is shown on the BBC's *Look* programme	Publication of Lester L. Short's *Woodpeckers of the World* by the Delaware Museum of Natural History: the first work to cover all species	Launch of Ohio space shuttle *Discovery* delayed for a month due to holes drilled in the craft by a northern flicker

2000 BC–AD 1500	1894–689 BC	9TH CENTURY BC

Mayan mythology includes references to woodpeckers, including how the earth goddess Chibirias painted the woodpecker's crest red

In ancient Persia and Mesopotamia wrynecks are considered close to the godhead and in Babylon a green woodpecker is associated with the goddess Ishtar

The Picenes establish Picenum in central Italy and a cult develops around a green woodpecker

1758	1861	1927	1940

In the tenth edition of his *Systema naturae* Carl Linnaeus (Carl von Linné) classifies 4,400 animal species, including many woodpeckers

The first major work on woodpeckers, Alfred Malherbe's four-volume *Monographie des picidées*, is published

The 'Yellowhammer' (northern flicker) is made the state bird of Alabama

Hollywood cartoon character Woody Woodpecker created by Walter Lantz

2000	2005	2006	2014

On 1 January the Central Bank of Suriname issue a five-gulden banknote with a red-necked woodpecker on the obverse

Ivory-billed woodpecker announced as 'rediscovered' in Arkansas in 2005; news makes the front page of the *New York Times*, but subsequent searches fail to find proof of its existence

Kaempfer's woodpecker is 'rediscovered' in Brazil after not having been seen for eighty years. Subsequent searches find more, although it is still classed as endangered

Publication of Gorman's *Woodpeckers of the World: The Complete Guide* by Bloomsbury. Published simultaneously as *Woodpeckers of the World: A Photographic Guide* by Firefly in North America

Appendix:
Woodpecker Species
Mentioned in the Text

Acorn woodpecker	(*Melanerpes formicivorus*)
American three-toed woodpecker	(*Picoides dorsalis*)
Andean flicker	(*Colaptes rupicola*)
Antillean piculet	(*Nesoctites micromegas*)
Arabian woodpecker	(*Dendrocopos dorae*)
Arizona woodpecker	(*Picoides arizonae*)
Ashy woodpecker	(*Mulleripicus fulvus*)
Bamboo woodpecker	(*Gecinulus viridis*)
Banded woodpecker	(*Chrysophlegma miniaceum*)
Bearded woodpecker	(*Dendropicos namaquus*)
Bennett's woodpecker	(*Campethera bennettii*)
Black-rumped flameback	(*Dinopium benghalensis*)
Black woodpecker	(*Dryocopus martius*)
Blond-crested woodpecker	(*Celeus flavescens*)
Chequer-throated woodpecker	(*Chrysophlegma mentale*)
Chestnut-coloured woodpecker	(*Celeus castaneus*)
Crimson-winged woodpecker	(*Picus puniceus*)
Cuban green woodpecker	(*Xiphidiopicus percussus*)
Downy woodpecker	(*Picoides pubescens*)
Eurasian green woodpecker	(*Picus viridis*)
Eurasian three-toed woodpecker	(*Picoides tridactylus*)
Eurasian wryneck	(*Jynx torquilla*)
Fernandina's flicker	(*Colaptes fernandina*)
Gila woodpecker	(*Melanerpes uropygialis*)
Gilded flicker	(*Colaptes chrysoides*)

Golden-fronted woodpecker	(*Melanerpes aurifrons*)
Great slaty woodpecker	(*Mulleripicus pulverulentus*)
Great spotted woodpecker	(*Dendrocopos major*)
Greater yellownape	(*Chrysophlegma flavinucha*)
Grey-headed woodpecker	(*Picus canus*)
Ground woodpecker	(*Geocolaptes olivaceus*)
Guadeloupe woodpecker	(*Melanerpes herminieri*)
Hairy woodpecker	(*Picoides villosus*)
Heart-spotted woodpecker	(*Hemicircus canente*)
Hispaniolan woodpecker	(*Melanerpes striatus*)
Imperial woodpecker	(*Campephilus imperialis*)
Ivory-billed woodpecker	(*Campephilus principalis*)
Jamaican woodpecker	(*Melanerpes radiolatus*)
Japanese woodpecker	(*Picus awokera*)
Javan flameback	(*Chrysocolaptes strictus*)
Kaempfer's woodpecker	(*Celeus obrieni*)
Lafresnaye's piculet	(*Picumnus lafresnayi*)
Lesser yellownape	(*Picus chlorolophus*)
Lewis's woodpecker	(*Melanerpes lewis*)
Magellanic woodpecker	(*Campephilus magellanicus*)
Maroon woodpecker	(*Blythipicus rubiginosus*)
Middle spotted woodpecker	(*Dendrocopos medius*)
Northern flicker	(*Colaptes auratus*)
Nubian woodpecker	(*Campethera nubica*)
Pale-billed woodpecker	(*Campephilus guatemalensis*)
Pale-headed woodpecker	(*Gecinulus grantia*)
Pileated woodpecker	(*Dryocopus pileatus*)
Puerto Rican woodpecker	(*Melanerpes portoricensis*)
Red-bellied woodpecker	(*Melanerpes carolinus*)
Red-breasted sapsucker	(*Sphyrapicus ruber*)
Red-cockaded woodpecker	(*Picoides borealis*)
Red-headed flameback	(*Chrysocolaptes erythrocephalus*)
Red-headed woodpecker	(*Melanerpes erythrocephalus*)
Red-naped sapsucker	(*Sphyrapicus nuchalis*)
Red-necked woodpecker	(*Campephilus rubricollis*)

Red-throated wryneck	(*Jynx ruficollis*)
Rufous piculet	(*Sasia abnormis*)
Rufous woodpecker	(*Micropternus brachyurus*)
Rufous-bellied woodpecker	(*Dendrocopos hyperythrus*)
Smoky-brown woodpecker	(*Picoides fumigatus*)
Southern sooty woodpecker	(*Mulleripicus fuliginosus*)
Speckle-chested piculet	(*Picumnus steindachneri*)
Stierling's woodpecker	(*Dendropicos stierlingi*)
Streak-throated woodpecker	(*Picus xanthopygaeus*)
Syrian woodpecker	(*Dendrocopos syriacus*)
Varzea piculet	(*Picumnus varzeae*)
West Indian woodpecker	(*Melanerpes superciliaris*)
White-bellied woodpecker	(*Dryocopus javensis*)
White-rumped woodpecker	(*Meiglyptes tristis*)
Williamson's sapsucker	(*Sphyrapicus thyroideus*)
Yellow-bellied sapsucker	(*Sphyrapicus varius*)
Yellow-faced flameback	(*Chrysocolaptes xanthocephalus*)
Yellow-fronted woodpecker	(*Melanerpes flavifrons*)
Yellow-shafted flicker	(*Colaptes auratus auratus*)

References

1 THE WOODPECKER FAMILY

1 Hans Winkler, 'Phylogeny, Biogeography and Systematics', in
   Developments in Woodpecker Biology, exh. cat., Biologiezentrum des
   Oberösterreichischen Landesmuseums, Linz, Austria (2015),
   pp. 7–35.
2 V. L. de Pietri, A. L. Manegold, L. Costeur and G. Mayr, 'A New
   Species of Woodpecker (Aves; Picidae) from the Early Miocene of
   Saulcet (Allier, France)', *Swiss Journal of Palaeontology*, CXXX (2011),
   pp. 307–14.
3 Albrecht Manegold and Antoine Louchart, 'Biogeographic and
   Paleoenvironmental Implications of a New Woodpecker Species
   (Aves, Picidae) from the Early Pliocene of South Africa', *Journal of
   Vertebrate Paleontology*, XXXII (2012), pp. 926–38.
4 H. Winkler, A. Gamauf, F. Nittinger and E. Haring, 'Relationships
   of Old World Woodpeckers (Aves: Picidae) – New Insights and
   Taxonomic Implications', *Ann. Naturhist. Mus. Wien, B*, CXVI (2013),
   pp. 69–86.
5 Matthew. J. Dufort, 'An Augmented Supermatrix Phylogeny of the
   Avian Family Picidae Reveals Uncertainty Deep in the Family Tree',
   Molecular Phylogenetics and Evolution, 94 (2015), pp. 313–26.
6 Josip del Hoyo, Nigel J. Collar, D. A. Christie, A. Elliott, L. D. Fishpool,
   *HBW and BirdLife International Illustrated Checklist of the Birds of the
   World*, vol. I: *Non-passerines* (Barcelona, 2014), pp. 610–88.
7 Gerard Gorman, *Woodpeckers of the World: The Complete Guide*
   (London, 2014).

8   Alexander F. Skutch, *Life of the Woodpecker* (Santa Monica, CA, 1985), pp. 93–7.
9   Richard N. Conner, D. Craig Rudolph and Jeffrey R. Walters, *The Red-cockaded Woodpecker: Surviving in a Fire-maintained Ecosystem* (Austin, TX, 2001).
10 Ernest Choate, *The Dictionary of American Bird Names* (Boston, MA, 1985).
11 Frank L. Burns, 'A Monograph of the Flicker *Colaptes auratus*', *Wilson Bulletin*, 31 (1900), pp. 1–82.
12 Jean-Michel Roberge and Per Angelstam, 'Usefulness of the Umbrella Species Concept as a Conservation Tool', *Conservation Biology*, XVIII (2004), pp. 76–85.
13 Raimo Virkkala, 'Why Study Woodpeckers? The Significance of Woodpeckers in Forest Ecosystems', *Ann. Zool. Fennici*, XLIII (2006), pp. 82–5.
14 M. C. Drever, K. E. Aitken, A. R. Norris and K. Martin, 'Woodpeckers as Reliable Indicators of Bird Richness, Forest Health and Harvest', *Biological Conservation*, CXLI (2008), pp. 624–34.

2 THE CARPENTER

1   Aristotle, *History of Animals*, trans. Richard Cresswell (London, 1862).
2   Pliny the Elder, *The Natural History of Pliny,* trans. John Bostock and H. T. Riley (London, 1857), books 10, 20.
3   Alexander Wilson, *An American Ornithology* (Philadelphia, PA, 1811), vol. IV, p. 23.
4   Lawrence Kilham, *Woodpeckers of Eastern North America* (New York, 1983).
5   Matti Kuusi, 'The Woodpecker That Helped People Out of the Tree', *Temenos: Studies in Comparative Religion*, IV (1969), pp. 67–75.
6   Thanks are due to Johnnie Kamugisha for this information from the 'old folks' in a village in Uganda.

7   Emiko Ohnuki-Tierney, *Illness and Healing among the Sakhalin Ainu: A Symbolic Interpretation* (Cambridge, 1981), p. 185.

8   Rendel J. Harris, 'The Voyage to Colchis of Jason', in *Boanerges* (Cambridge, 1913), p. 228.

9   Aristophanes, *The Birds and Other Plays*, trans. Alan H. Sommerstein and David Barrett (London, 2003), p. 193.

10 L. J. Gibson, 'Woodpecker Pecking: How Woodpeckers Avoid Brain Injury', *Journal of Zoology*, CCLXX (2006), pp. 462–5.

11 J. P. McCurrich, *Leonardo da Vinci: The Anatomist* (Washington, DC, 1930).

12 Hans Winkler, David Christie and David Nurney, *Woodpeckers: A Guide to the Woodpeckers, Piculets and Wrynecks of the World* (Robertsbridge, 1995), pp. 16–19.

13 Sang-Hee Yoon and Sungmin Park, 'A Mechanical Analysis of Woodpecker Drumming and its Application to Shock-absorbing Systems', *Bioinspiration and Biomimetics*, VI (2011).

14 H. and V. Winkler, 'The Brains of Woodpeckers', in *Developments in Woodpecker Biology*, exh. cat., Biologiezentrum des Oberösterreichischen Landesmuseums, Linz, Austria (2015), pp. 55–61.

15 Ibid.

16 G. K. Gajdon and H. Winkler, 'Cognition in Woodpeckers', in *Developments in Woodpecker Biology*, pp. 63–76.

17 T. B. Oatley, 'Going to Ground: The Life of a Terrestrial Woodpecker', *Africa: Birds and Birding*, VIII/5 (2003), pp. 29–33.

18 Gerard Gorman, 'Identifying the Presence of Woodpecker (*Picidae*) Species on the Basis of Their Holes and Signs', *Aquila*, CII (1995), pp. 61–7.

3 THE DRUMMER

1   Gerard Gorman, *The Black Woodpecker: A Monograph on Dryocopus martius* (Barcelona, 2010), pp. 40–44.

2   Fannie Hardy Eckstorm, *The Woodpeckers* (New York, 1901), p. 15.

3 D. J. Dodenhoff, R. D. Stark and E. V. Johnson, 'Do Woodpecker Drums Encode Information for Species Recognition?', *The Condor*, CIII (2001), pp. 143–50.

4 Gerard Gorman, *Woodpeckers of the World: The Complete Guide* (London, 2014). These descriptions of drumming are from several species accounts in the book.

5 Richard N. Conner, D. Craig Rudolph and Jeffrey R. Walters, *The Red-cockaded Woodpecker: Surviving in a Fire-maintained Ecosystem* (Austin, TX, 2001), p. 171.

6 Heinz Sielmann, *My Year with the Woodpeckers* (London, 1959), p. 26.

7 Eckstorm, *The Woodpeckers*, pp. 16–17.

8 Ibid., p. 55.

9 Gorman, *The Black Woodpecker*, p. 42.

10 Fray Ramón Pané, *An Account of the Antiquities of the Indians: Chronicles of the New World Encounter*, trans. Susan C. Griswold (Durham, NC, and London, 1999), chap. VIII, p. 12.

11 Jacob Grimm, *Teutonic Mythology*, trans. James S. Stallybrass (Cambridge, 2010), vol. III, p. xxxii.

4 THE MYTHICAL WOODPECKER

1 Plutarch, *Plutarch's Lives*, trans. John Dryden (New York, 2008), vol. I, p. 39.

2 Ovid, *Ovid's Fasti*, trans. Betty Rose Nagle (Indianapolis, IN, 1995), book 3, p. 82.

3 Ernst and Luise Gattiker, *Die Vögel im Volksglauben* (Wiesbaden, 1989).

4 Aristophanes, *The Birds and Other Plays*, trans. Alan H. Sommerstein and David Barrett (London, 2003), p. 171.

5 Francis Celoria, *The Metamorphoses of Antoninus Liberalis* (London and New York, 1992).

6 Antony Clare Lees, *The Cult of the Green Bird: The Mythology of the Green Woodpecker* (Lancaster, 2002), p. 21.

7 Strabo, *The Geography of Strabo*, trans. Horace Leonard Jones (Cambridge, MA, 2014), vol. I, chap. 4.

8 Ovid, *Fasti*, p. 82; Plutarch, *Lives*, p. 39.

9 Plutarch, *Moralia*, trans. Frank Cole Babbitt (London, 1936), answer to Roman question 21.

10 Athenaeus of Naucratis, *Deipnosophistae*, 9. 369.

11 Plutarch, *Moralia*, answer to Roman question 21.

12 Virgil, *The Aeneid*, trans. David West (London, 2003), p. 142.

13 Ovid, *Metamorphoses*, trans. David Raeburn (London, 2004), pp. 565–7.

14 Robert Graves, *The White Goddess* (Manchester, 1999), p. 469.

15 Dionysius, *The Roman Antiquities of Dionysius of Halicarnassus*, trans. Earnest Cary (London, 2015), p. 33.

16 R. J. Wheeler, 'Metal Crested Woodpeckers: Artifacts of the Terminal Glades Complex', *Florida Anthropologist*, L (1997), pp. 67–81.

17 Clarence B. Moore, 'Certain Aboriginal Remains along the Black Warrior River', *Journal of the Academy of Natural Sciences Philadelphia*, XIII (1905), pp. 125–244.

18 Henry W. Hamilton, 'The Spiro Mound', *The Missouri Archaeologist*, XIV (1952).

19 Wilson Duff, ed., *Histories, Territories and Laws of the Kitwancool* (Victoria, BC, 1959).

20 W. L. McAtee, 'Trade Value of the Beak of the Ivory-billed Woodpecker', *Condor*, XLIV (1942), p. 41.

21 Thomas Buckley, *Standing Ground: Yurok Indian Spirituality, 1850–1990* (Berkeley, CA, 2002), p. 208.

22 E. W. Gifford, 'Southern Maidu Religious Ceremonies', *American Anthropologist*, XXIX (1927), pp. 214–57.

23 Pliny Earle Goddard, *Hupa Texts* (Berkeley, CA, 1904), pp. 207–14.

24 Timothy Jordan, 'Reciprocity and Hupa Woodpeckers', *California Cultures: A Monograph Series*, II (2012).

25 Joseph Bruchac, *Native American Animal Stories* (Golden, CO, 1992), pp. 63–6.

26 Shepard Krech III, *Spirits of the Air: Birds and American Indians in the South* (Athens, GA, 2009).

27 George A. Dorsey, *Traditions of the Caddo* (Lincoln, NE, 1997), pp. 94–5.

28 Richard Rhodes, ed., *The Audubon Reader* (New York, 2006), p. 109.

29 Alex Barker, 'Early Uses of the Ivory-billed Woodpecker', *Science*, CCCIX (2005), p. 1814.

30 J. Murphy and J. Farrand, 'Prehistoric Occurrence of the Ivory-billed Woodpecker (*Campephilus principalis*), Muskingum County, Ohio', *Ohio Journal of Science*, LXXIX (1979), pp. 22–3.

31 A. M. Bailey, 'Ivory-billed Woodpecker's Beak in an Indian Grave in Colorado', *Condor*, XLI (1939), p. 164.

32 Paul W. Parmalee, 'Additional Noteworthy Records of Birds' Archaeological Sites', *Wilson Bulletin*, LXXIX (1967), pp. 155–62.

33 J. Eric S. Thompson, *Maya History and Religion* (Norman, OK, 1970), pp. 206, 350–52.

34 Noel F. R. Snyder, David E. Brown and Kevin B. Clark, *The Travails of Two Woodpeckers: Ivory-bills and Imperials* (Albuquerque, NM, 2009), p. 92.

35 Bruchac, *Native American Animal Stories*, pp. 67–72.

36 C. Marius Barbeau, *Huron and Wyandot Mythology: With an Appendix Containing Earlier Published Records* (London, 2013), p. 77.

37 Fray Ramón Pané, *An Account of the Antiquities of the Indians: Chronicles of the New World Encounter*, trans. Susan C. Griswold (Durham, NC, and London, 1999), chap. VIII, p. 12.

38 Fellow woodpecker enthusiast Thomas Hochebner supplied me with these gems of information.

39 Steve Froemming, 'Traditional Use of the Andean Flicker (*Colaptes rupicola*) as a Galactagogue in the Peruvian Andes', *Journal of Ethnobiology and Ethnomedicine*, II (2006), p. 23.

40 Fanny Hagin Mayer, *Ancient Tales in Modern Japan* (Bloomington, IN, 1985), p. 265.

41 Claude Lévi-Strauss, *The Naked Man: Mythologiques*, trans. J. and D. Weightman (Chicago, IL, 1990), vol. IV, p. 493.

42 Ibid., p. 214.

43 Ibid., p. 464.

44 Carl Lumholtz, *Unknown Mexico: A Record of Five Years' Exploration Among the Tribes of the Western Sierra Madre* (Cambridge, 2011), vol. II, pp. 107–8.
45 Kevin Strauss, *Tales with Tails* (London, 2006), pp. 184–5.
46 Paul Schebesta, *Among the Forest Dwarfs of Malaya* (Kuala Lumpur, 1973).
47 J. R. Swanton, *Tlingit Myths and Texts* (Washington, DC, 1909).
48 Miguel Ángel Palermo, *La Victoria de Kákach* (Buenos Aires, 2008).
49 Hitakonanu'laxk, *The Grandfathers Speak: Native American Folk Tales of the Lenape People* (New York, 1994), pp. 97–8.

5 THE MAGIC WOODPECKER

1 Frank J. Lipp, *The Mixe of Oaxaca: Religion, Ritual and Healing* (Austin, TX, 1991), p. 29.
2 John E. Staller and Brian Stross, *Lightning in the Andes and Mesoamerica* (Oxford, 2013), p. 168.
3 Jacob Grimm, *Teutonic Mythology*, trans. James S. Stallybrass (New York, 2004), vol. II, p. 675.
4 Ernst and Luise Gattiker, *Die Vögel im Volksglauben* (Wiesbaden, 1989).
5 Rendel J. Harris, *Picus Who Is Also Zeus* (Cambridge, 1916).
6 I am grateful to Alain Fossé for information on woodpeckers as rain birds in France and for his translations.
7 Ingvar Svanberg, *Fåglar i svensk folklig tradition* (Stockhom, 2013).
8 W. B. Lockwood, *The Oxford Book of British Bird Names* (Oxford, 1984), pp. 172–3.
9 Elias Owen, *Welsh Folklore: A Collection of the Folk-tales and Legends of North Wales* (Oswestry, 1896).
10 J. H. Reichholf, 'Der mysteriöse "Gießvogel"', *Mitteilungen der zoologischen Gesellschaft Braunau*, IX (2005), pp. 53–60.
11 I'd like to thank Jiří Horáček for this background from Bohemia and his translations from the Czech.
12 Fellow woodpecker enthusiast Paul Harris kindly provided me with this translation of an Italian dialect.

13 Lockwood, *British Bird Names*, pp. 26, 171.

14 Fellow woodpecker enthusiast Thomas Hochebner supplied me with this gem of information.

15 J. R. Swanton, *Tlingit Myths and Texts* (Washington, DC, 1909).

16 Frank L. Burns, 'A Monograph of the Flicker *Colaptes auratus*', *Wilson Bulletin*, XXXI (1900), pp. 1–82.

17 Kenneth W. Noe, ed., *The Yellowhammer War: The Civil War and Reconstruction in Alabama* (Tuscaloosa, AL, 2014).

18 James Henry Breasted, *Ancient Times: A History of the Early World* (Boston, MA, 1916).

19 U. Perktas, G. F. Barrowclough and J. G. Groth, 'Phylogeography and Species Limits in the Green Woodpecker Complex (Aves: Picidae): Multiple Pleistocene Refugia and Range Expansion across Europe and the Near East', *Bio. Journ. Linn. Soc.*, CIV (2011), pp. 710–23.

20 Rendel Harris, 'The Woodpecker and the Plough', in *Boanerges* (Cambridge, 1913), pp. 205–15.

21 Antony Clare Lees, *The Cult of the Green Bird: The Mythology of the Green Woodpecker* (Lancaster, 2002), p. 79.

22 Gregory Mawar, 'Iban Cultural Heritage', www.gnmawar. wordpress.com, 16 December 2015.

23 Sonia Tidemann and Andrew Gosler, eds, *Ethno-ornithology: Birds, Indigenous Peoples, Culture and Society* (London, 2010), p. 110.

24 Ernst and Luise Gattiker, *Die Vögel im Volksglauben* (Wiesbaden, 1989).

25 I am grateful to Gehan Rajeev for this information from rural Sri Lanka.

26 I'd like to thank Uku Paal for this fascinating snippet from Estonia.

27 I am grateful to Hans Winkler for these explanations and translations.

28 Jacob Grimm, *Teutonic Mythology*, trans. James S. Stallybrass (New York, 2004), vol. II, p. 673.

29 Kevin Strauss, *Tales with Tails* (London, 2006), pp. 115–16.

30 Irinia L'vovna Zheleznova, *Tales of The Amber Sea: Fairy Tales of the Peoples of Estonia, Latvia and Lithuania* (Moscow, 1987).

31 Carl Jacob Bender, *Tales from the Jungle* (Girard, KS, 1924), pp. 12–13.

32 I am grateful to Hans Winkler for digging this snippet up.

33 Max Rendle, 'Studien und Kritiken zur Naturgeschichte des Schwarzspechtes *Picus martius*', in *Die Gefiederte Welt*, XLIII (1914); Kurt Loos, *Der Schwarzspecht: Sein Leben und seine Beziehungen zum Fortsthaushalte* (Vienna and Leipzig, 1910).

34 Irene Würdinger, 'Spechte in Mythen, Sagen und im Brauchtum', *Beih.Veröff. Natursch. Landschaftspfl. Baden-Württemberg*, LXVII (1993), pp. 27–32.

35 Ellen C. Babbitt, *Jataka Tales* (Radford, VA, 2008).

36 Sunita Parasuraman, 'The Duel between Elephant and Sparrow', in *The Panchatatantra* (Mumbai, 2011).

37 Svetlana Annenkova kindly translated this Russian folktale for me.

38 Aleksandr Afanas'ev, *Russian Fairy Tales* (New York, 1973), pp. 199, 499–500.

39 Matti Kuusi, 'The Woodpecker That Helped People Out of the Tree', *Temenos: Studies in Comparative Religion*, IV (1969), pp. 67–75.

40 Gerard Gorman, *Woodpeckers of the World: The Complete Guide* (London, 2014), pp. 359–61.

41 Steve Froemming, 'Traditional Use of the Andean Flicker (*Colaptes rupicola*) as a Galactagogue in the Peruvian Andes', *Journal of Ethnobiology and Ethnomedicine*, II (2006), p. 23.

42 Pliny the Elder, *The Natural History of Pliny*, trans. John Bostock and H. T. Riley (London, 1857), books 10, 20.

43 Barbara Diamond Goldin, *The Family Book of Midrash: 52 Jewish Stories from the Sages* (Plymouth, 2006), pp. 26–31.

44 Jacob Grimm, *Teutonic Mythology*, trans. James S. Stallybrass (Cambridge, 2010), vol. III, p. 937.

45 Pliny, *Natural History*, 27, 60.

46 Hildegard von Bingen, *Physica*, trans. Priscilla Throop (Rochester, VT, 1998), pp. 193–4.

47 Emiko Ohnuki-Tierney, *Illness and Healing among the Sakhalin Ainu* (Cambridge, 1981), pp. 49, 193.

48 Claude Lévi-Strauss, *The Savage Mind* (Chicago, IL, 1966), p. 9.

49 M. R. Harrington, 'Sacred Bundles of the Sac and Fox Indians', *University of Pennsylvania Museum of Anthropology Publications*, IV (1914), pp. 123–262.

50 Carl Lumholtz, *Unknown Mexico: A Record of Five Years' Exploration Among the Tribes of the Western Sierra Madre*, vol. II (Cambridge, 2011).

51 Ernst and Luise Gattiker, *Die Vögel im Volksglauben* (Wiesbaden, 1989).

52 This Vietnamese tale, taught in school, was related to me by Le Quy Minh.

53 Betty Mindlin, *Unwritten Stories of the Suruí Indians of Rondonia* (Austin, TX, 1995), pp. 62–5.

54 Tidemann and Gosler, *Ethno-ornithology*, p. 110.

55 Froemming, 'Traditional Use of the Andean Flicker', p. 23.

6 WOODPECKERS TODAY AND TOMORROW

1 J. W. Fitzpatrick et al., 'Ivory-billed Woodpecker (*Campephilus principalis*) Persists in Continental North America', *Science*, CCCVIII (2005), pp. 1460–62.

2 BirdLife International, species factsheet *Campephilus principalis*, www.birdlife.org, December 2015.

3 Both quotations from Rick Wright, 'Taking It Personal: Where the Ivory-bill Survives', *Birding* (March/April 2007), pp. 48–52.

4 Jerome Jackson, 'Ivory-billed Woodpecker (*Campephilus principalis*): Hope, and the Interfaces of Science, Conservation, and Politics', *Auk*, CXXIII (2006), pp. 1185–9.

5 Don Thomas, *Orbit of Discovery: The All-Ohio Space Shuttle Mission* (Akron, OH, 2014).

6 Anon, 'War on the Red-headed Woodpecker', *Osprey* (July–August 1987), p. 147.

7 P. Fayt, M. M. Machmer and C. Steeger, 'Regulation of Spruce Bark Beetles by Woodpeckers: A Literature Review', *Forest Ecology and Management*, CCVI (2005), pp. 1–14.

8 W. D. Koenig, A. M. Liebhold, D. N. Bonter, W. M. Hochachka and J. L. Dickinson, 'Effects of the Emerald Ash Borer Invasion on Four Species of Birds', *Biological Invasions*, xv (2013), pp. 1–9.

9 C. K. Vishnudas, '*Crematogaster* Ants in Shaded Coffee Plantations: A Critical Food Source for Rufous Woodpecker *Micropternus brachyurus* and Other Forest Birds', *Indian Birds*, iv (2008), pp. 9–11.

10 Throughout this chapter I have used the threat level terms and codes of the iucn Red List of Threatened Species, www.iucnredlist.org/about/introduction.

11 A. R. Styring and M.Z.B. Hussin, 'Effects of Logging on Woodpeckers in a Malaysian Rain Forest: The Relationship between Resource Availability and Woodpecker Abundance', *Journal of Tropical Ecology*, xx (2004), pp. 495–504.

12 R. T. Pinheiro and T. Dornas, 'New Records and Distribution of Kaempfer's Woodpecker *Celeus obrieni*', *Revista Brasileira de Ornitologia*, xvi (2008), pp. 167–9.

13 Gerard Gorman and Chris Sharpe, 'Globally Threatened Bird: Speckle-chested Piculet *Picumnus steindachneri*', *Neotropical Birding*, xvi (2015), pp. 18–19.

14 James T. Tanner, 'The Decline and Present Status of the Imperial Woodpecker of Mexico', *Auk*, lxxxi (1964), pp. 74–81.

15 Tim Gallagher, *Imperial Dreams: Tracking the Imperial Woodpecker through the Wild Sierra Madre* (New York, 2013).

16 T. Jogahara, G. Ogura, T. Sasaki, K. Takehara and Y. Kawashima, 'Food Habits of Cats (*Felis catus*) in Forests and Villages and Their Impacts on Native Animals in the Yambaru Area, Northern Part of Okinawa Island, Japan', *Honyurui Kagaku (Mammalian Science)*, xliii (2003), pp. 29–37 (in Japanese with an English abstract).

Select Bibliography

Backhouse, Frances, *Woodpeckers of North America* (Buffalo, NY, 2005)

Bent, Arthur Cleveland, *Life Histories of North American Woodpeckers* (Indianapolis, IN, 1992)

Clare Lees, Antony, *The Cult of the Green Bird* (Lancaster, 2002)

Eckstorm, Fannie Hardy, *The Woodpeckers* (New York, 1901)

Estrada, R. Alberto, *Looking for the Ivory-billed Woodpecker in Eastern Cuba* (Create Space Independent Publishing Platform, 2014)

Gallagher, Tim, *Imperial Dreams: Tracking the Imperial Woodpecker through the Wild Sierra Madre* (New York, 2013)

—, *The Grail Bird* (New York, 2005)

Gorman, Gerard, *The Black Woodpecker: A Monograph on Dryocopus martius* (Barcelona, 2011)

—, *Woodpeckers of Europe: A Study of the European Picidae* (Chalfont St Peter, 2004)

—, *Woodpeckers of the World: The Complete Guide* (London, 2014)

Hoose, Phillip, *The Race to Save the Lord God Bird* (New York, 2004)

Jackson, Jerome A., *In Search of the Ivory-billed Woodpecker* (New York, 2004)

Kilham, Lawrence, *Woodpeckers of Eastern North America* (New York, 1983)

McFarlane, Robert W., *A Stillness in the Pines: The Ecology of the Red-cockaded Woodpecker* (New York, 1992)

Malherbe, Alfred, *Monographie des picidés* (Metz, 1861)

Ritchison, Gary, *Downy Woodpecker* (Mechanicsburg, PA, 1999)

Short, Lester, *Woodpeckers of the World* (Greenville, DE, 1982)

Shunk, Stephen A., *Peterson Reference Guide to Woodpeckers of North America* (New York, 2016)

Sielmann, Heinz, *My Year with the Woodpeckers* (London, 1959)

Skutch, Alexander F., *Life of the Woodpecker* (Santa Monica, CA, 1985)

Snyder, Noel F. R., David E. Brown and Kevin B. Clark, *The Travails of Two Woodpeckers: Ivory-bills and Imperials* (Albuquerque, NM, 2009)

Tanner, James T., *The Ivory-billed Woodpecker* (New York, 1942)

Tekiela, Stan, *Remarkable Woodpeckers* (Cambridge, MN, 2011)

Villard, Pascal, *The Guadeloupe Woodpecker* (Brunoy, 1999)

Winkler, Hans, David A. Christie and David Nurney, *Woodpeckers: A Guide to the Woodpeckers, Piculets and Wrynecks of the World* (Robertsbridge, 1995)

Associations and Websites

AUDUBON GUIDE TO NORTH AMERICAN WOODPECKERS
www.audubon.org/bird-family/woodpeckers

CAMEPEPHILUS WOODPECKERS
http://cwoodpeckers.blogspot.com

WOODPECKERS OF EUROPE (blog)
http://woodpeckersofeurope.blogspot.com

WOODPECKERS OF THE WORLD (blog)
http://woodpeckersoftheworld.blogspot.com

WOODPECKERS OF THE WORLD (Facebook group)
www.facebook.com/groups/1438058619755392

WWF ADOPT A WOODPECKER
http://gifts.worldwildlife.org

Acknowledgements

Thank you to Michael Leaman, Jonathan Burt, Harry Gilonis and Jess Chandler at Reaktion. I am very grateful to Simon Cook, Peter Powney and Rick Wright, who read early drafts of the text and helped me hammer and chisel it into shape, and to Hans Winkler in Vienna for his expert input on many woodpecker matters. Thanks, too, to Jairo Sanchez Porras and Jennifer Pickering of Leaf Community Arts in Costa Rica, and to Will Meadows and the Ainu Community of Nibutani, Hokkaido. Muchas gracias to Israel Guzmán, Javier Hernandez and Robinson Rosado for background on the Taíno. Danny Alder, Svetlana and Vaughan Ashby, Neil Bowman, Josef Chytil, Bill Duyck, Con Foley, Alain Fossé, Paul Harmes, Paul Harris, Christina Hart-Davies, Erik Hirschfeld, Uditha Hettige, Thomas Hochebner, Jiří Horáček, Le Quy Minh, Martin Hrouzek, Markus Jais, Kevin Jones, Alf King, Rein Kuresoo, Alex Lees, Seppo Leinonen, Donna Martin, Lee Mott, Uku Paal, Sam Pacenovsky, Sandra Paci, Tatiana Petrova, Gehan Rajeev, Lia Rosenberg, Gerhard Rotheneder, Lars Smith, Noel Snyder, Antero Topp, Stephan Weigl and Christian Zurek, also all helped in innumerable ways. Thanks again.

Photo Acknowledgements

The author and publishers wish to express their thanks to the below sources of illustrative material and/or permission to reproduce it. Some locations uncredited in the captions for reasons of brevity are also given below.

Photo Daniel Alder: p. 95 (foot); photo Ambroix: p. 140 (top left); photos Vaughan Ashby: pp. 66, 94; from John James Audubon, *The Birds of America*, vol. IV (Philadelphia, PA, 1840): pp. 36, 78, 81, 128; photos by or courtesy of the author: pp. 6, 9, 13, 17 (right), 18, 19, 22, 23, 25, 26, 29, 30, 40, 41, 44, 47, 48, 49, 55, 57, 58, 61 (top right), 84, 85, 86, 96, 97, 101, 103, 108, 113, 114, 115, 126, 129, 132, 139, 141, 142, 144, 146, 147, 148, 150; photos Neil Bowman: pp. 17 (left), 42, 46, 69 (foot); British Library, London: p. 117; Brooklyn Museum, New York: p. 76 (foot); photo Daderot: p. 76 (top left, top); photo Bill Duyck: p. 116; F l a n k e r has released the work at the top left of p. 68 into the public domain (this applies worldwide, but, as in some countries this may not be legally possible, in such cases F l a n k e r grants anyone the right to use this work for any purpose, without any conditions, unless such conditions are required by law); photo Con Foley: p. 106; Gitanyow National Historic Site, British Columbia: p. 77 (left); from John Gould, *Birds of Asia*, vol. V, parts XXV–XXX (London, [1873–7] 1850–83): p. 20; from John Gould, *The Birds of Europe* (London, [1832–]7): p. 109; from John Gould, *The Birds of Great Britain*, vol. I (London, 1862): p. 72 (photo courtesy of The New York Public Library – www.nypl.org); photo Carrie Griffis: p. 79; photos Paul Harris: pp. 68 (top right), 69 (top right); photo Christina Hart-Davies:

Index

176